The Digitterran Tsunami

The Digitterran Tsunami

Web 3.0 and the Rise of the NEO Citizen

Volume I:

The Twenty-One Principles Driving the Evolution of the Web

By Dele Atanda

Library of Congress Control Number: 2013908766
CreateSpace Independent Publishing Platform
North Charleston, SC

Dele Atanda can be followed @DigiTTsu or @DeleAtanda

Dedicated to Tunde,

who inspired me to see the world differently,

and to Lulu who gives me the courage to try and change it.

Contents

Part 2 NEO Citizens

- The Five Dimensions of NEO-Citizenship Rights
- NEO-Citizenship—Values and Principles
- The Decline of the Nation-State
- The Rise of the Virtual State

Part 3 The Historic Context

- The Information Revolution
- The Knowledge Revolution
- Web 1.0
- Web 2.0

Preface

I once read in a book on Internet start-ups that if you are not a little embarrassed by the first release of your product then you have probably released it too late. I think the same thinking can also be applied to creative and literary works. I originally wrote this book in 2009 under the title of *The Aquarian Tsunami*. In the spirit of Web 2.0 projects, I published it as a series of posts in a blog at www.aquariantsunami.com, inviting feedback from friends and colleagues. Suffice to say I was a little embarrassed by some elements of the book.

In 2009, when I wrote *The Aquarian Tsunami,* the global economic system had fallen into a deep recession and the second decade of the millennium was approaching. Though a dysfunctional and overleveraged banking system was seen as the cause of the current bust cycle, as opposed to the overinflated Internet stock valuations blamed for the recession of 2000, there are similarities between the global social climate now and the one that gave birth to the Web 2.0 phenomenon. However, conditions currently are more extreme than they were at the turn of the millennium. There is in fact an exponential acceleration in the current pace of change compared with the 2000s. This cycle's financial crisis has been more catastrophic and intense than the previous one. Similarly, the transformations brought by the third wave of Internet innovations will be more disruptive and world changing than those brought by second-generation ones such as social media and peer-to-peer computing.

In 2009 it was clear to me that the Internet would facilitate a new social-political awakening and accelerate social-political change. I stated then that governments would fall before the end of the financial crisis. My predictions have been vindicated by the well-documented upheavals in what has come to be known as the Arab Spring. This, if anything, has given me greater conviction and determination in publishing this work, for I am now confident that the transformations that this book and its subsequent volumes foretell are only just getting started. I believe a new type of citizen is emerging, increasingly empowered and self-assured, and that before the current social economic upheaval has settled, nations will fall and the geopolitical boundaries of the world will change significantly as a result. I believe we are seeing a new social, political, and cultural world order being born—or a *new earth order* (NEO), as I call it—driven by new citizens, NEO-citizens, empowered by technology, demanding a new type of society and new types of intrasocial relationships. I have outlined in this book the twenty-one core principles I believe to be driving this transformation. Future volumes will show how technology underpinned by these principles will reshape our societies, values and lives.

Based on feedback from friends and colleagues and on developments in the offing, I have retitled the book *The Digitterran Tsunami.* I have moved the historic section to the end of the book and brought the principles upfront to the beginning. I have changed all previous *Aquarian* references to *Digitterran* in line with the new title and have also added a section, "The Rise of the Virtual State," to chapter 2. Aside from this and some minor prose refinements and grammatical corrections, the work remains the same as it was when first published in 2009.

The original works can still be seen as a series of posts at www.aquariantsunami.com.

I emphasize this, as many people have asked me if this work remains relevant four years later and if it is possible to predict with any credibility how the digital phenomenon will unfold. It is my belief that there are twenty-one fundamental principles driving the digital revolution—twenty-one principles that are clear, predictable, and indisputable. It is for this reason that I wrote this work in the first place. Furthermore, what is startling after revisiting the work after four years is not only how accurate these predictions have proved to be but how increasingly relevant and poignant they have become.

It is my view that the Digitterran Tsunami is just getting started and that the twenty-one principles outlined herein will continue to drive the digital revolution well into the next decade. It is what I call my 2020 vision. For what it is worth, I feel this is an important vision to share and humbly hope that it inspires a handful of NEO-citizens to rise on this wave and shine.

As for me, I will continue to develop this work in various formats with the intention of contributing toward and expediting the arrival of the Digitterran era.

Dele Atanda

January 2013

Overview

The first part of this book defines the twenty-one core principles that are driving the next wave of Internet innovations and its corresponding superwave of social-political change, or Digitterran Tsunami as I am calling it. The second part defines a new type of citizen—the NEO-citizen who will emerge as a result of these Web 3.0 opportunities.

Chapter 3, the last part of the book looks at the evolution of the Internet and attempts to provide a consolidated view of its role in the information and knowledge revolutions, contextualizing it from the vantage point of general social evolution. It shows how the World Wide Web emerged from the Internet and how it eventually evolved into the Web 2.0 phenomenon we are familiar with today. It also outlines the key principles of Web 2.0, explaining what differentiates it from Web 1.0.

Those less interested in the historical perspective or those familiar with the background of the Internet's evolution may want to skip the last chapter.

Introduction

There has been much written in recent years on the second generation of Internet technologies and the phenomenon otherwise known as Web 2.0. Many technologists within the Internet industry dislike the term *Web 2.0*, citing that the Internet is a constantly evolving medium or that Web 2.0 is merely a marketing term. It is even said that Web 2.0 is really Web 1.0 simply understood by the wider corporate world. While all of these points have differing degrees of validity, it cannot be denied that the term *Web 2.0* has helped explain and facilitate a shift in the minds of people, corporations, and governments in seeing the Internet as a major social, cultural, and commercial phenomenon. Tim O'Reilly of O'Reilly Consulting coined the term *Web 2.0* in the aftermath of the stock market crash of 2001, often referred to as the "dot bomb." He used it to explain how the Internet would rise from its ashes in a second wave of innovation and business-value creation as companies embraced the technology as a business platform, exemplified by some notable enterprises such as Amazon, eBay, Google, and others.

So powerful has been the adoption of the term *Web 2.0* into contemporary corporate vernacular that most companies that have not done so already are now looking at the web and its second-generation models as key technological challenges to understand and decode in order to remain relevant and competitive in their industries. The power of the web and its second-generation tools has become undeniable as a major force of change in the consumer landscape with the rise of social networks and user-generated media typified by companies such as Facebook and YouTube and the clamor of big companies to engage consumers through these channels. "Being part of the conversation happening between consumers," "engaging consumers where they congregate," and "enabling user participation" are all terms and plans that can be found in the digital strategies of all of the most progressive and powerful companies on the planet today.

Even the once-traditional and orthodoxy-entrenched political landscape has become irreversibly changed by the indisputable power of using second-generation Internet culture and tools to influence, engage, and mobilize people to action, as evidenced in the recent US presidential elections. Web 2.0 has truly now come of age, and the world is now paying attention to how powerful a platform the Internet is as a tool for accelerating cultural, commercial, and social change.

However, many are aware that the revolution that the Internet represents is nascent at best, that we are still very much at the embryonic stage of this epic journey and that rapid and radical changes typify the path being laid out by this phenomenon. As such, some are starting to question what the next wave of innovation and changes in the Internet will bring. What will Web 3.0 look like, and what transformations will it bring to our world and current notions and expectations?

This book and its following volumes attempt to answer that question by providing a glimpse into a world not so far away from the one in which we live currently, a world that will see ever-closer integration between the Internet and our daily lives, a world in which we will become truly immersed in our digital experiences. It in fact goes further to suggest that our world is poised to being swept by a third wave of Internet innovation, a wave that will be so deep, expansive, and far-reaching that it is more appropriate to view it as a superwave—a wave in fact so super that all nations and societies struck by it will be left dramatically changed in its wake. So dramatic will be this destruction of the old and creation of the new that this wave might be better understood as a sort of tsunami of change—a tsunami of innovation, creativity, and technology that will sweep away much of the world models we know currently and leave us all submerged in a new web of empowered and engaged citizens living in a digitally enabled, planetary meritocracy that is multicultural, multipolarized, and ecologically active.

A world beginning at the dawn of this decade where people are interconnected with people and where things are interconnected with things to keep people connected. An ecosystem enshrined in a pervasive and immersive digital web, enabling a planetary renaissance of creativity and productivity driven by collaboration and innovation. A *Webbed-Wide-World* swept in by a tsunami of invention and imagination, a tsunami driven and enabled by a collective desire for a different and better world, a Digitterran Tsunami of evolution and change.

Emerging from the debris of this tsunami's wake will be a new type of consumer, a new type of citizen of a new social order or *new earth order* (NEO), as I am calling it. This new citizen or NEO-citizen will be a more empowered, socially active, and ecologically balanced than the citizen we see today. NEO-citizens will be vocal, influential, and connected to a global network of like-minded citizens—citizens who are restless for change and for a better world and who are aware of the power and pace of the tsunami that has liberated and empowered them. This ever-increasing network of awakened NEO-citizens combined with the revolutionary opportunities accorded by the Digitterran Tsunami will represent an unstoppable force for social, cultural, and political change in the world. Together they will create movements that begin in the virtual world but that rapidly spill out into the physical world, irreversibly changing it in ways that cannot yet be imagined.

This book and subsequent books in this series tell the story of such citizens and the story of the digital wave upon which they ride. It outlines twenty-one core principles driving this phenomenon. Seven of these principles relate to information exchange and flow, seven to social and organizational structures, and seven to the ethical and philosophical frameworks guiding the phenomenon. The Digitterran Tsunami is a call to action for citizens, enterprises, and governments of the world to embrace this powerful wave of change and with it bring forth a new era of innovation, prosperity, and social advancement.

The Coming of a New Age

The Digitterran Tsunami is a cultural technological movement that will usher in a new social-political paradigm on our planet. It will represent a quantum leap in our social evolution as a species and will transform the norms of our world.

There have been many references to major changes in our social order over the ages accounted for in different ways in mythology, astrology, and science. Invariably some have been more imaginative than others. It is important to contextualize these changes around a vision of what most people would like to see change in our current world. A vision that speaks to a technologically advanced world founded on higher human values of balance, fairness, and ecological harmony. As the technical limitations of our machines recede it will become increasingly important that we code higher values into their workings such as ethics, justice, and compassion for them to benefit us all holistically. The Digitterran Tsunami rises from this convergence of technology, social awareness and cultural momentum.

Digitterra itself translates from Digital Terra (Earth) and refers to a digital world that overlays and augments our physical one. The Digitterran era represents the period of cultural, social and political evolution driven by the increasingly seamless flow of information between our physical and digital worlds into services that can be used to drive changes in our environments and lives. It began with the information revolution and gained pace with the arrival of the Internet and will accelerate exponentially over the next decade as the web's third wave of innovation rises. The Digitterran Tsunami is the swell of innovation, creativity and change rising as the expansion of this digital earth takes on a more central and essential role in our lives and societies. It highlights the evolutionary potential of our societies, an important input into the global psyche and digital mind that will drive the innovations of the next digital wave in a direction that benefits mankind and our planet as a whole, countering the more dystopian views of potential futures that will become inevitable if we do not balance them with progressive alternatives.

However, in order for the Digitterran Tsunami to usher in a more balanced and optimistic future, it will need to be powered by an energy within the masses that congregates around a vision of and belief in a better world. This belief will drive people to action and innovations that create the changes they wish to see. There will be many catalysts and advocates of this vision and many different tools that will bring incremental advances along the way, but a shared belief in a different and better world will be the heart of the momentum of this movement. There are notable writers to whom I will refer within this book, such as Alvin Toffler with his seminal work on *The Third Wave,* Kenichi Ohmae and his work on *The Borderless World,* Kevin Kelly with his work on *The First Five Thousand Days of the Internet,* as well as others who have written on the changing paradigm the world is currently experiencing, providing insight into the world that awaits us beyond this shift. Though the vision laid out here aggregates and builds on several such movements and world views, I will refer to the drivers for this social evolution henceforth as Digitterran drivers in line with the vision of a Digitterran era. I have identified twenty-one core principles driving this phenomenon and will describe each in detail. I will focus on how the Internet enables and amplifies these principles and accelerates the changes they command. Therefore when I refer to the Digitterran Tsunami I refer to the wave of social, cultural, and political change sweeping our world driven by twenty-one key principles, underpinned by people's quest for a better world for themselves and their peers, enabled by global advances in information communication technologies that bring about a new era in our social cultural evolution as a species on planet Earth.

Summary of the Waves of the Internet

Web 1.0	Web 2.0	Web 3.0
Culture		
Mass Markets	Long Tail	Epicentres
Internationalisation	Globalisation	Planetarianism
Consumer Connection	Consumer Engagement	Consumer Enablement
Rich Media	Rich Experiences	Shared Experiences
Brochureware	Web Services	Micro Applications
One-Way Communication	Bilateral Communication	Multi-Polar Communication
Repurposed Content	User-Generated Content	Co-created Content
Campaigns	Conversations	Movements
New Media	Social Media	Converged Media
Brand Message	Brand Immersion	Multi-Polar Brands
Brand Ownership	Brand Influence	Co-Branding
Interactive	Social	Shared
Surf/browse	Converse/create	Co-create/ contribute

Web 1.0	Web 2.0	Web 3.0
Text/Images	Video/Audio	Events/Experiences
Virtual Reality	Virtual Worlds	Augmented Experience
All Rights Reserved	Some Rights Reserved	Distributed Rights
Control	Cooperation	Codependency
Personal Computers	Personalised Content	Personalised Internet
Chat Rooms	Social Networks	Virtual States
World Wide Web	Social Web	Webbed Wide World
E-commerce	Social Commerce	Social Services
Information		
Finding Info	Sharing Info	Shaping Info
Static Content	Dynamic Content	Intelligent Content
Database Driven	Enriched Data	Interconnected Data
Commercial		
E-commerce	Social Commerce	Social Services
Monopolies	Native Net	Multi-Polar

Web 1.0	Web 2.0	Web 3.0
Technology		
Technical Centricity	Social Centricity	Human Centricity
Bandwidth	Broadband	Ever-Presence
Closed Networks	Open Networks	Ecosystems
Algorithmic Search	Social Search	Semantic Search
Proprietary	Open Source	Co-owned
Connected PCs	Connected People	Connected Tribes
Rapid Development	Perpetual Beta	Continuity
Operating Systems	Interoperability	Interdependence
Programs	Algorithms	Neural Networks
Network to Network	Peer to Peer	Tribe to Tribe
Presentation versus Content	Content versus Context	Context versus Meaning
HTML/Flash/ JavaScript	Ajax/XML/HTML5	SPARQL/OWL/RDF
Processing Power	Social Power	Imaginative Power

Part I

Chapter 1   The Twenty-One Digitterran Principles

The Digitterran Tsunami is being driven by twenty-one key principles that underpin the technical, social, and cultural changes of this third wave of Internet innovations. These principles are grouped into three sets of seven principles. One set governs how information is structured, one set relates to how we organize ourselves as people and societies, and the final set focuses on the ethical and philosophical issues driving the tsunami.

The Seven Information Principles

The first seven principles of the Digitterran Tsunami outline the changes in information organization that will drive the Internet's evolution.

1.1   Granularity

The first Digitterran principle we will explore is granularity. The idea here is that the next decade will bring an unprecedented degree of granularity in how we approach information, people, and organizations. In the twentieth century, the approach to media and marketing communications between organizations and people was a mass broadcast one. A single message or set of messages was transmitted to many people via television, print, or radio. Most people were exposed to the same messages as other people in their localities or nations. In the case of "world news" and information, a handful of multinational media companies, such as the BBC, News Corporation, Time Warner, and CNN, were able to broadcast single messages to multiple nations. All in all though, the model was one message or group of messages going out to many people.

Similarly in the manufacturing sector, one product or range of products was designed and mass-produced by a few and sold to many people across local, national, and global markets. Thus we can see the dominant industrial and media communication models of the twentieth and early twenty-first centuries have been ones of mass production and mass broadcast. Henry Ford is generally credited with founding mass production from his automobile production lines, though there is some evidence of mass production in ancient China. Mass production and mass communication enabled companies to achieve huge economies of scale and to centrally develop goods and content in a standardized way that could be sold over and over again. The mass-production model enabled companies to sell the same product in many international markets, thereby facilitating their expansion into international businesses. Needless to say, the model led to huge profits for companies that managed to exploit it well.

In the 1980s and 1990s, however, an idea—led by Joseph Pine—of customizing and localizing mass-produced goods emerged as a popular concept with management theorists. Companies began to realize that while they achieved significant economies of scale by producing generic, mass-market products, they encountered problems when selling these products and services if they were not localized in some sort of way for consumer tastes and needs in particular markets. The idea that mass-produced goods could be modified in ways that enabled the economic benefits of mass production to be realized while delivering the sales traction associated with products more closely aligned to local markets was at the heart of this thinking. The model became known as mass customization. It required companies to have a more granular understanding of their markets and to modify their products to reflect the differences between the markets in order to be successful in them.

Personalization was the next step in the evolution of this thinking. Localized products could be further customized according to individual consumer tastes or needs. This enabled consumers to add their own requirements to the production cycle, enabling mass-produced goods that could be customized to personal requirements. Examples of such customization are the wide variety of color, trim, and finish options that car manufacturers are able to provide customers or the configuration of computers that buyers can specify with companies such as Gateway 2000 and Dell. BMW ran a campaign in recent years where it offered customers the opportunity of having their car's paint matched to any color of their choosing. If the customer could provide the color, BMW would match it. Toyota's successful Scion brand also developed cars targeted at Generation Y consumers that could be configured and customized in a wide variety of ways to meet differing customer needs for expression and personalization.

Some industries and companies have been more successful than others in achieving mass customization. Overall, the idea poses a significant challenge to the mass-production industrial model prevalent since the industrial revolution. This is because mass production thrives on uniformity and on delivering the same product over and over again. Customization and personalization are diametrically opposed to this thinking. They require the management of multiple variables and options. The two approaches are therefore difficult to effectively align. All the same, mass customization is becoming increasingly necessary for many products to remain relevant and attractive to modern consumers. This is representative of the trend toward ever-increasing granularity in the market. Macro "one size fits all" solutions are becoming increasingly difficult to deploy successfully. Businesses and organizations have to segment and target their consumers in much more granular and micro terms than they have had to do to date.

The Web 2.0 environment has brought an even greater need to personalize customers' experiences of service offerings, following on from the trend of mass customization and personalization seen in the industrial sector. That said, the personalization we see online today in the form of personalized greetings when one visits a web page or personalized versions of web pages are still very rudimentary in their degree of granularity and personalization compared with what we are going to see in the next decade. The idea of mass customization and a growing celebration of autonomy and individuality in the consumer psyche are driving a need to approach consumers in a much more targeted and tailored manner. This means that organizations need to have a much more granular understanding of their customers in order to gain their attention and custom.

Granularity really represents a shift away from approaching people as massive blocks of consumers defined by extremely simple and generalized demographic or psychographic information to an approach where people are seen more as individuals with diversified qualities, needs, and requirements.

Granularity represents a need to communicate and connect with people in this manner, as they demand greater recognition of their diversity and uniqueness.

Information in the web is going to become much more granular than it is currently. This is the idea behind a popular Web 3.0 concept: the semantic web. We will explore the idea of the semantic web in detail later in this series, but for now a quick overview is needed.

The principal theory behind the semantic web is that data will effectively be linked more closely to data as opposed to more generally to pages. To explain this a little further, one can effectively say that the precursor to the Internet as we know it today was a world of separate computer networks connecting a handful of computers with each other. These were mostly closed private networks with computers physically wired to each other. The Internet came into being by connecting these separate networks into a single, logical, virtual network of networks. This was primarily achieved with a "packet switching" protocol that allowed information to flow seamlessly from one network to another. Thus a virtual *internetwork* of computers was conceived and created by allowing networks of interconnected computers to talk to each other. This was the Internet at its base definition and is how the medium was born.

The World Wide Web soon came along and became a means of connecting pages of information on different computers with other pages of information on other machines within the one logical network. Through hyperlinks (links to different computer files) and HTML (Hypertext Markup Language), we could basically make connections between pages sitting on different computers through a browser. What is interesting is that in the evolution of local networks of computers into the Internet and the Internet into the World Wide Web, processes of granularity occurred. We first went from computer-to-computer links in closed, physical networks, to network-to-network links in an open virtual network—the Internet that broke up the physical networks of groups of computers by assimilating them into one logical network of all interconnected computers. With the World Wide Web, we then went to a more granular relationship between pages of content on different machines linking with pages of content on other machines. It no longer mattered on what machines the pages were or what networks those machines were within. Those two lines of demarcation became irrelevant, and a more granular relationship between pages of information and people consuming them became more important than the computers on which the information resided or the networks in which the computers sat. The World Wide Web effectively became a ubiquitous computer with a ubiquitous network. This was a concept that many companies of the Web 1.0 era did not understand. They sought to create closed private networks within the Internet and control people's access to content within and outside of those networks as per the early Internet. Examples were the early AOL network, the CompuServe network, the MSN Network, etc., as mentioned before. Needless to say, all of these closed network models failed. The only ones that managed to succeed were those that changed their model and adopted an open access approach to the web.

In the early days of the Internet, Microsoft was so convinced that closed systems were the way forward that Bill Gates publicly denounced the World Wide Web for being too open a medium in 1995, advocating Microsoft's closed private network, the Microsoft Network, as the way forward. The Microsoft strategy was to funnel all traffic to the Internet through MSN, which the company could control. As such, it bundled MSN with Windows 95 so consumers could access the Internet via MSN easily from within Windows. AOL and CompuServe had similar ambitions with their networks.

These closed network models all failed, and the only entities to survive were those that changed their models to open system. Microsoft, realizing the folly of the closed network approach, sought to control access to the Internet via the next best thing, the web browser. This resulted in it developing Internet Explorer and launching the browser wars in the famous United States vs. Microsoft class action of 1998, led by the US Department of Justice. Netscape and others claimed Microsoft was monopolizing the market by bundling its Internet Explorer browser with its Windows 95 operating system. While Microsoft prevailed to win the browser war against Netscape and its Navigator, the 1995 market leader and first truly multiplatform browser, its market dominance has since been eroded by a collection of emerging browsers, including Mozilla's Firefox, Google Chrome, Safari, and Opera.

The semantic Web 3.0 concept is that our Internet system will evolve to link data directly with data intelligently to provide people with aggregated and more useful information. That means that if I look at a particular page on a website and there is a word in there, it will link to words related to that word on other machines. Say, for example, I select the word *culinary*. Then the computer or the web will be able to understand that that word relates to food, which relates to seasoning and relates to restaurants and relates to this whole cluster of terms that are similar or that have a related meaning. This will be regardless of whether the word *culinary* is on a food-related page or not. This is not the case with the web today. With today's web, associations can be made only between pages, not between the data within the pages.

Therefore the semantic web no longer simply becomes about the links between computers or the links between pages that contain content, but it becomes about links between content itself at a very micro level. This could be at the level of a sentence, at the level of a word, at the level of a video, at the level of a cluster of information, at the level of an idea, or at the level of a theory; the examples go on in perpetuity.

The important thing to note is there will be a much more granular relationship between things in the web. There will be a much more granular relationship between content, between people and organizations, between organizations themselves, and between nations and regions. The web's content will be broken down or "atomized" to its smallest components, and connections between these components will be made at the micro (data) level. This will facilitate a much richer, relevant, and intuitive informational experience for web users. We can see how the more open linking of pages to pages as opposed to linking networks to networks or machines to machines has led to a much richer Web 2.0 world versus a more rigid and controlled Web 1.0 world. This phenomenon will increase exponentially when we can link data directly with data.

Granularity will also be evident at a personal level. The reason people's social profiles and search and browsing habits have become of such great interest to search engine companies, Internet service providers, and social networks is so they can build complex pictures of individuals. The more granular data an organization can gather about a consumer, the better equipped it will be at tailoring products and services to the individual's needs and desires. This complex picture of an individual will make that individual unique. There will be a hypergranularity of bits of information within a person's profile that go to make the profile itself. This combination of multiple bits of often disparate data and the relationships among these data elements will make people's profiles ever more complex and nebulous. The more granular the information, the more complex the profile can become and the more effective targeting models can be at reaching such people with content and information that is of interest to them.

The granularity in the components of data that form a person's profile will be one thing, but there will also be granularity in terms of people's interaction among themselves. That is to say that people will be understood and grouped via much more granular and complex models than the demographic or psychographic models used to target people currently. People will group together into ever-increasingly specialized and niche interest groups. This is because Web 2.0 and Web 3.0 technologies will enable them to find each other and bond. Organizations that understand this and engage with their audiences as such will be much more successful than those that do not.

So we can see that granularity will have an impact at the content, data, and informational levels as we have explained. We have also seen that it will drive changes at the consumer and personal level, where we will see a much greater degree of customization and personalization. There will also be greater granularity in the groups and networks that people form. The granularity and diversity of the individuals of these networks will be a principle, as will be the granularity of networks themselves. We will start to see a greater proliferation of microcommunities forming around niche subjects and interests.

This is a continuation of the Web 2.0 idea of the long tail, coined by Chris Anderson and discussed in chapter 3. It proposes that you can have numerous pockets or niches of people that group together for a variety of reasons. However, in order to reach these niche, long-tail groupings, communicators—be they commercial, political, or social—will have to atomize their messages so that their message elements can be combined to fit a wider range of audiences than they have targeted in the past. It is sort of like a Lego system. One can create many more objects by providing the base building blocks of multiple objects rather than complete objects themselves. It is difficult to build new objects if one cannot break down a complex object into its constituent parts. However, if one can, one can continuously create new, interesting, and relevant objects from a set of base building blocks. That is to say, communication messages will need to be much more granular and configurable, so that they can be adapted to have resonance with a wider range of different groupings. The same will be the case with manufacturing and production. This is a principle that is at odds with twentieth-century mass-production and mass-media communications but one that is going to vastly increase in the 3.0 Digitterran era.

Finally we will also see granularity in the technology space. We will see an increasing emergence of microapplications and services. This will be particularly pronounced with social technologies. Theses microapplications will be available through collaboration and open source development networks, enabling people to combine them to create useful and entertaining services that can be consumed and distributed via the Internet. As with information, the atomization of applications and programs will enable a fertile environment for innovation and growth.

1.2   Ever-Presence

The second Digitterran principle we will discuss is that of ever-presence. In the Digitterran era, we will move toward a state where the Internet becomes much more integrated into our lives. It will become more integrated because it will be more ubiquitous and ever present. It will be around us everywhere, and we will be able to access it at any time. It will also become more integrated because of its incredible reliability. Futurist Kevin Kelly of *Wired* magazine describes the Internet as "the most reliable machine man has ever created." It has never failed, crashed, or been down. Individual machines, servers, and browsers have, but the whole machine never has, and barring an electricity blackout across the whole planet, it is unlikely that it ever will. Even if the unthinkable event were to happen, alternative power sources are likely to keep the Internet functioning. This, after all, is the purpose for which it was originally created, as a military defence system that would enable packet switching[1] or communication among networks in the event of a primary network failure.

With the pervasion of technologies such as Wi-Fi[2] and WiMAX,[3] we are already starting to see cities around the world—for example, Kuala Lumpur in Malaysia, London in the United Kingdom, and Salt Lake City, Utah, in the United States—developing prototypes of citywide permanent access through WiMAX networks for anyone, anywhere in the city, at anytime.

The web being available to us at anytime, wherever we are, is going to be a key principle of the next wave of the Internet.

This will bring a significant change in how we use the Internet, because it's going to bring about a sense of reliability and dependability on the Internet in providing us with services. Having

---

[1] Packet switching is a rapid store-and-forward networking design that divides messages into arbitrary packets, with routing decisions made per packet. Early networks used message-switched systems that required rigid routing structures prone to single point of failure. This led Paul Baran's US military-funded research to focus on using packet switching to include network redundancy, which in turn led to the widespread urban legend that the Internet was designed to resist nuclear attack.—Wikipedia.

[2] Wi-Fi is a trademark of the Wi-Fi Alliance for certified products based on the IEEE 802.11 standards. This certification warrants interoperability among different wireless devices.

[3] WiMAX (Worldwide Interoperability for Microwave Access) is a telecommunications technology that provides up to 3Mbits/s wireless transmission of data and Internet access.

the Internet accessible at all times is going to drive cultural changes in how we interface and work with the web.

We can already see examples of this now. Our reliance on cell phones as a means of always being able to get in touch with people is a fascinating trend of our era. This means the need to make stringent arrangements when meeting up with people has changed dramatically in the past ten to fifteen years. Since we know we can always reach people on the go, we can now make much more fluid plans and, if necessary, call, text, or e-mail to make last-minute changes. So there are significant cultural changes in terms of how we socialize, meet, and bond with people as a result of this.

Again, the pervasion of GPS services, not only in automotive navigation but also on cell phones, means that it's very easy for us to find our way to places now. All we need is an address from someone to find our way to them. No longer is there a need to plan a route or get detailed directions before we set out. This trend will take on a much more dramatic turn as we move into the Digitterran era.

The ever-presence of the Internet is going to lead to an evolution of a significant amount of services. An example of a field in which we might see dramatic changes would be health care. A recent article in the US press spoke of the first Wi-Fi-enabled pacemaker to be issued to a US patient. This Wi-Fi-enabled pacemaker allowed the patient's doctor to monitor the patient's heart remotely, 24/7. The patient, though initially uncomfortable with the invention, became increasingly comforted with the knowledge that their heart was under constant surveillance. The doctor was also excited about the development as it meant he could spend less time collecting basic data from routine tests and more time on research and understanding how to improve his patient's condition. So we can see in the Digitterran era the prospects of our vital statistics and medical state being monitored reliably and constantly over the Internet. We will be able to depend on the Internet to make a connection between a patient and a doctor that is permanent and ever-present. The implications of this for the elderly and those at regular risk with medical conditions are considerable. We are likely to see a greater prevalence of this sort of ever-present health monitoring for citizens in countries and regions with aging populations, such as Japan and Europe.

Another area where the ever-presence of the Internet might start to drive major social and cultural changes is in developing markets that often have interrupted electricity supplies. Communication and entertainment pretty much grinds to a halt in such markets... except for via cell phones. With the emergence and proliferation of solar smartphones in such markets with broadband connections, we can see that the web, via portable devices, will be a more reliable means of communicating, entertaining, and distributing media to such markets than television or even radio.

Also, things like augmented reality will make significant advances around this idea of ever-presence. We are already seeing evidence of this in some parts of the developing world where the fact that the Internet is ever-present means people can document and leave virtual notices for people in virtual, geo-spatial locations that can provide critical information on development or aid work that has been done in an area. This means it is easier for new workers or supporters to understand the problems of an area and pick up relevant information on previous work done or on projects yet to be completed with time and special sensitivities by simply connecting with virtual notes left by others.[4] This can create myriad forms of opportunities through new means of recording and accessing information and affecting people's lives based on permanent digital infrastructures, which can always be accessed and updated.

We can also think about burglar systems, alarm systems, and all sorts of connections to emergency services that can be facilitated through the ever-presence of the Internet. We will start to see more life and operations-critical systems designed around the ever-presence of the Internet.

We will also start to see things like automated grocery systems. For a long time, there has been the idea of the smart refrigerator, which when down on supplies can communicate with you. So when you are in a supermarket, your refrigerator will be able to communicate what's in it and what has been finished or is low via the ever-present web.

Real-time access will be another benefit of this ever-present Internet. The fact that the Internet will be ever-present will drive more real-time information flow between people and organizations. The ever-presence of the Internet and its ubiquity will mean that we will be able to interact with the system in a much more real-time manner than we can do currently.

---

[4] See Diagram: http://appfrica.net/blog/2009/08/12/the-future-of-giving/#utm_source=rss&utm_medium=rss&utm_campaign=the-future-of-giving.

Again, this is going to bring a significant change in the mind-set of developers, programmers, and application providers, and also from consumers in what we expect from the Internet. The fact that the Internet is ever-present and completely accessible will change the way we look at many current services. Take telephone conversations, for example. The idea that telephone conversations should be restricted by cost will quickly become redundant because of the ever-present infrastructure of the Internet. Since our voices are just another form of data that is being passed along the net, the idea of paying a separate fee for this data service will become increasingly odd.

1.3   Interconnectedness

An important principle that will gain momentum in the Digitterran era is interconnectedness. This interconnectedness in itself will have a couple of nuances to it. We have already discussed the interconnectedness that will emerge among data with the semantic web. Additionally we will start to see a great degree of interconnection between things. The next decade will usher in an Internet-connected world; it's what some call the *Internet of Things* or what I call the *Webbed Wide World*. At base level things like our cars, telephones, televisions, refrigerators, and homes are going to become web-enabled. They will all have a means of communicating with us, their owners, through the Internet. In this sense most of the objects of our lives will start to have digital tags and codes that enable us to identify and communicate with them. Our clothes, keys, books, and possessions will all become web-enabled and identifiable in cyberspace. Also, our digital world will become much more closely overlaid onto our real world. These worlds will increasingly converge. As such, the web will become a much more three-dimensional and even four-dimensional space, as there will also be a time element to the location of things. Where things are in time and space will become very easy to map in this interconnected, ever-present web that is coming. Whether these things are our keys, wallets, handbags, or whatever, most will have some form of signature or digital component that will enable us to track, trace, monitor, and even move them via the Internet. This will change things significantly. I gave the example earlier of groceries that are automatically replaced as you consume things from your refrigerator. As something leaves one point and goes to another—from the refrigerator to the garbage can, for example—there is the potential for the appliance to communicate directly with the supermarket and autoreplenish it should you choose that, or for it to send a reminder to your virtual shopping list, letting you know you need this. Interconnectedness, however, is going to become much more profound than this.

We are also going to become much more interconnected with each other. Six degrees of separation are very few when you have a digitally connected world. We are going to become much more interconnected with our networks of friends, colleagues, and associates than we have been, as is already apparent through social networking facilities such as LinkedIn, Myspace, HiPiHi, etc. A great example of this is a recent collaboration between the *Huffington Post* and Facebook called Huffpost Social News. The application tracks which articles its readers are reading, commenting on, and voting on and then posts details onto the reader's friends' Facebook pages. As such friends know what other friends are reading about and are interested in, allowing them to keep in sync with each other without even discussing these interests together. This becomes a powerful way for people to discover content that may be of interest to them that they may not have previously discovered, as articles posted in their Facebook feeds are of interest to their friends, with whom they are likely to share common interests. What makes the Huffpost Social News application so profound is that the sharing is automated and widely distributed. It builds on the notion that reading and watching news is an inherently social process. It stimulates discussion, debate, and even action. This sharing of information is part of the appeal and success behind blogging and microblogging. Also, this personalization of the news raises our friends' level of interest in it. Hence we all become catalysts in informing of our friends and bringing information to their attention. The roles that we play in our networks as discoverers, conduits, and filters of information therefore become much more profound and seamless, and our connections with each other potentially become much more meaningful and enriching through this technology.

1.4   Living Data

In the Digitterran era, we will see data at the heart and core of all things. The next wave of the web is very much going to be data-centric. We will discuss the semantic web specifically in the next volume, as well as the relationship between data and data, which we touched on briefly before, but for the purpose of this principle suffice to say the Digitterran era is going to be focused on data. Data is effectively going to become the electricity that drives the engine of the next wave of the Internet. Owing to semantic intelligence, data will become increasingly intelligent in and of itself, making it much more dynamic and interrelated. This will become so powerful that data will start to take on a life of its own and become more of a living, animate-like substance than a simple informational one.

In the United Kingdom, legislation has been introduced that allows companies to have their databases of consumers, products, and suppliers, etc., added to the assets of their balance sheets. So data is taking a very real and tangible position within the valuation of corporate assets in the world today. The understanding of data though, its importance and value, is going to increase much further than this. Data is going to occupy one of the highest positions of value in the Web 3.0 value chain. We already see this in the often-cited showdown between Google and Facebook in our current Web 2.0 world. There is clearly a real race by both of these organizations to aggregate as much data about consumers as possible. Google develops tremendous applications and great capabilities that it distributes to the market via a free or minimal-cost model. One of the essential reasons why Google does this is because it is hungry for data about its consumers and their world. The more it understands about its consumers, as we have discussed, the better Google will be able to target services to them. In terms of personalization and getting accurate and relevant information to consumers, data is the key enabler. Additionally, data will build relationships between data itself, between people, between organizations, between objects, and within the whole ecosystem. Data will effectively become the electrons or atomic elements with which we will be able to build complex applications and services. Data will be the most granular and fundamental element flowing through the system.

Also, as the physical and virtual worlds converge, we will start to see all things as expressions of data. If you look at all material objects at the molecular level, atomic information is data. Even biological, physiological, and some psychological qualities can now be understood as expressions of genetic data. This has great implications when we look at disciplines such as nanotechnology, chemical engineering, and biogenetics. At the micro, medium, and macro levels, all things are expressions of data. Whether that is quantum data, molecular data, geo-location data, biometric data, behavioral data, or interactive data, all things will be expressed as data. The Internet will allow us to correlate and observe interrelationships among data from these three perspectives and exploit it across all in unprecedented ways. This will be one of the key principles we will see in the Digitterran era.

As we have said, data will be a currency of the twenty-first century. I believe there will be several key currencies that emerge in the Digitterran era. Examples would include social currencies, eco-currencies, and engagement currencies. But all of these currencies will be underpinned by the fundamental value of the data that supports them, similarly to how modern currencies were underpinned by commodities.

The history of modern money essentially consists of three phases. The first phase was commodity money whereby actual valuable commodities were bartered in trade. The second was representative money in which paper notes were used to represent precious commodities, usually gold, that were stored elsewhere. The notes could be exchanged for the equivalent commodity at any time. This practice began in

China in the ninth century and became what was known as the gold standard when adopted by other countries around the world. The final form of currency was the fiat money system in which paper notes were backed by the use of "lawful force and legal tender laws" of the government issuing the currency. The fiat system was historically used only during times of war, during which it was normal for governments to suspend the convertibility of promissory notes into commodities. After the wars, governments usually reverted back to the gold standard.

After the Second World War though, Britain found it had depleted its gold reserves and led a campaign to establish an International Monetary Fund via the 1944 Bretton Woods Agreement. This was a system based on the convertibility of various national currencies into US dollars that in turn were convertible into gold. Via the same Bretton Woods Agreement, many governments linked their currency's value relative to the US dollar. The US government agreed to fix the price of gold to a value of thirty-five dollars per ounce. So all currencies that were fixed to the dollar were indirectly but effectively pinned to the price of gold. In the 1970s under the system, French President Charles de Gaulle reduced France's dollar reserve, trading it in for US gold in an attempt to reduce America's influence on international commerce. This, coupled with America's overextension in the Vietnam War, dramatically affected US economic potency, resulting in President Nixon eliminating the fixed gold price in 1971 and causing the whole system to collapse. Since then the global economic system has reverted to a fiat monetary system backed only by use of "lawful force and legal tender laws" of the governments to enforce value and market forces as determined by the international foreign exchange system.

International trading information and macroeconomic data, combined with "lawful force and legal tender laws," determine the value of currencies in today's international money markets. It is therefore fair to say that data is currently at the heart of currency valuation.

There are interesting theories around the devaluation of currency in the current economic meltdown, having to do with the absence of a gold standard or a representative commodity, such as petroleum, to which a tangible value can be attached to currencies. Also, gold itself as a commodity has reached record trading prices as confidence in the dollar as the global reserve currency falters in the markets.

All currencies in the Digitterran era will be underpinned by data, only more explicitly than they are now. As mentioned previously, new forms of currency will evolve around engagement, social capital, and ecological indices. Data will be the fundamental building block through which value is attributed to these and traditional forms of currency, and data will become increasingly central to our money exchanges. Data in itself will become a form of currency, as it will have commercial value that can be traded and exchanged with other currencies. We will also start to see data-driven economies and data-driven commerce.

As I have said, the tangible world will become expressions of data, and so too will the intangible worlds. Interactions, as we mentioned, will become expressions of data. Engagement will become expressions of data. Sensibilities, happiness, and joy will all have data representations in the digital world, and there will be this constant strife and yearning to quantify intangible things, experiences, and sentiments, whether they be sorrow, pleasure, sadness, frustration, excitement, etc., as expressions of data. The Internet as a system will crave this information in itself, and organizations will crave this information in order to be able to assess, judge, and understand their customers. People will also crave this information to have a better understanding of themselves. Therefore, data as an expression of intangibles is another phenomenon we will see become poignant with Web 3.0.

In the Digitterran era, not only will data be central to all things, but data will also be a catalyst for change. Data will become more than just a representation of things. Data will actually drive significant changes in the complete social landscape. Data will become increasingly capable of understanding data itself, enabling it to self-organize itself into information. This self-organizing feature will transform data from being disparate and static to being interconnected and dynamic, bringing it to life in a sense. This living data will become much more effective and prolific in driving change. We will start to see, for example, data-driven activism. The more information becomes available to people, the more aware they will become of things happening around them and the more they will take action. Also, the more they can see that their action causes changes and results, the more inspired they will be to take further action.

An old adage in the business world is what gets measured, gets done. This also seems to be true in our personal worlds. The digital world gives us a means through which we can measure things. The more we measure things, the more we pay attention to things, the more information we can derive from our measurements, the more it will catalyze behavioral changes and alterations in the way that we approach things. So data as a catalyst, as a dynamic quality that drives economic, social, cultural, and physical change, is going to be a key principle of the Digitterran era. As we will explore later, data-driven observations will also become central in other areas, such as in the worlds of science, theory, and philosophy, all of which will also be significantly touched by data-centricity. Not only will all things be quantified and expressed in data forms and not only will data expressions permeate all things, but data in itself will become a key catalyst to change.

1.5   Convergence

Another major Digitterran principle is convergence. This principle too has several dimensions to it. One of these is the continuation of the Web 2.0 principle of interoperability. The core idea behind interoperability is that anything that comes into the Internet system should be able to talk with the system as a whole, and any part of the system should be able to talk with it. There will continue to be a great need for interoperability among systems, devices, and applications in a Web 3.0 world—even more so than there has been to date. It will be a basic requirement of all systems in the digital world. Interoperability is going to become crucial for any organization, application, or service that appears on the Internet. There will still be proprietary data and proprietary restrictions around many things, but the idea of separate platforms will disappear. We are seeing this in the Web 2.0 world, where, for example, the operational disparity between the world of Apple Mac computers and PC computers has effectively disappeared. Both systems still have fundamental differences, but they are much more interoperable. A Mac user can communicate and share content with a PC user in a way that was much more difficult if not impossible ten years ago.

This trend is going to play out most dramatically in the fields of rich media content and mobile devices. Some sort of standards will emerge for content formats, enabling them to be consumed across all systems so that all of our systems can interoperate as one system. Our cars will be interoperable with our phones, with our computers, with our televisions, with our houses, with our refrigerators, with our office PCs, etc.

The idea of the web as a digital platform that can consume any form of content and serve content to any form of digital device will become increasingly prevalent and powerful. Publishers will need to generate products and content in ways that they can be consumed by or connected to anything that requests to do so, as long as the entity or person has the right privileges—whether that be a person, a device, an object that needs to extract information from it, an application, another piece of content, or whatever. Interoperability between things, between systems, objects, and devices, is going to be a key component of the success of the next wave. The need for that will drive a whole group of standards and stabilization methodologies to ensure that devices and systems can talk with each other easily.

The futurist Kevin Kelly put forward a wonderful concept that when you actually add up the plethora of different connections that we have to the Internet at the moment, it is in fact more beneficial to look at the Internet as a single machine.[5] It is actually one system, one machine—a machine that has had zero downtime in the mere five thousand or so days that it has been with us. He proposes that it is a single entity and that all the connections to it form part of that single machine. All the cameras, cell phones, keyboards, and other input devices are its eyes, ears, and senses, and all of its output devices are its voice, hands, and creative limbs. This is a very useful model through which to view the digital world and an important vantage point from which to view the principle of convergence. The Internet has become this all-consuming, ever-present, single machine. This machine has multiple touch points and sensory connections with all of us as people. As such within the machine itself, there is and will be a drive for the convergence of all its systems, platforms, applications, and devices. All of these must be able to talk seamlessly to each other, via each other, in order for the single machine to be able to work efficiently and effectively. Very much like a human brain, there are all these separate nodes of activity within the web, but it is the connectivity between theses nodes and the transportability of information, content, data, or electricity from one node of the system to another that makes it this brilliant organ that is able to develop rich concepts and theories, etc. The one-machine idea really emphasizes the principle of convergence of the Internet, that all systems, all

---

[5] www.youtube.com/watch?v=J132shgliuY&feature=related

applications, and all devices will converge into this one machine and that we too will converge to interface with it.

Again, there must be a convergence of data and a convergence of content in order for the machine to be able to serve media to its users in various guises and places and with various requirements and devices. We are going to see a convergence of media and also a convergence of platforms. So mobile platforms will have to converge with personal computer, television, IPTV, radio, and camera platforms. All silos of media will need to converge so that content can move freely from any part of the system to another and be consumed by us, in any which way we want, through multiple devices and multiple interfaces. A convergence of media and platforms will be necessary to facilitate this. Organizationally, there will also be a convergence of systems within enterprises—a convergence of external- and internal-facing systems, of HR systems, of accounting systems, of payment systems, of value chain systems, of logistic systems, and customer relationship management systems. All of these separate silos will need to converge in order for the machine to process this information and to extract the value from it that organizations and we as consumers require from it. Systems convergence will therefore be another key trend we will see in the Digitterran Tsunami.

We will also see a convergence of more tacit features. For example, we will start to see through the web a convergence of culture. Kenichi Ohmae, in his seminal books on borderlessness, globalism, and the new global paradigm, talks about what he calls *Californiaization*. His concept is that so many people around the world consuming American and Hollywood culture is creating a kind of generic global culture. Middle-class consumers in Tokyo probably share more in common with middle-class consumers in Los Angeles, London, and New York than they do with blue-collar workers in Kanazawa in Japan. This is because they consume very similar media, travel to similar places, and have similar aspirations and lifestyles as middle-class Californians. This common lifestyle and exposure to common media is driving the *Californiaization* trend Ohmae identifies. As I highlight in the multipolarity principle, I don't believe that it will be as mono-dimensional or monolithic as it has been in the late twentieth century, but there will most definitely be a convergence of international cultures. And there will be a convergence of communities, whether these are at the social networking level, at the peer-to-peer level, at the local or national level, or at the global, regional, or international level. We will start to see a convergence of communities, a convergence of localities, and a convergence of countries.

Already, we see this model working with the big blocks that are starting to become more and more prevalent and effective around the world, such as the European Community (EC) in Europe, the North American Free Trade Agreement (NAFTA) in the North Americas, the African Union (AU), the Southern African Development Community (SADC), and the Economic Community of West African States (ECOWAS) in Africa, Oceania in Asia, the G8, the G20, the United Nations, the OECD, etc. The convergence of nations and the convergence of the interests of nations is a trend we will see continue.

We will also see the convergence of organizations. We are not talking in the classic sense of mergers and acquisitions here, but more in the sense of a convergence of operations and resources. As borders start to disappear between organizations, the people within them will converge more, whether this is formally acknowledged with new corporate entities or not. There will be a greater convergence in the way that organizations operate. They will have to do so to remain relevant to consumers as their needs and tastes become increasingly discriminating, complex, and demanding.

We will also see the convergence of disciplines. Most intellectual and academic disciplines are currently highly demarcated and operate in silos. However, owing to the ability of the Internet to deliver collaborative, multipolar tools and perspectives on issues, we will start to see much more diversified teams tackling problems and looking for solutions to issues. This is going to lead to a convergence of disciplines. In order to solve an ecological problem, we will involve a variety of disciplines. In order to solve a security problem, we might end up with anthropologists, chemists, linguists, and theorists, along with psychologists and nutritionists, involved in finding a solution. The Internet will enable us to converge our disciplines much more constructively and creatively. It will dissolve the need to differentiate those disciplines when applying them to solving problems, unless such divisions help find a solution.

We are therefore also going to see a convergence of theories. We can already, for example, see the disciplines of biology, genetics, and genetic engineering merging with the disciplines of nanotechnology and information technology. This kind of convergence between the theories of separate fields and the disciplines of these fields has already begun, and we will see more of this convergence as we go forward.

In the same way that the codes, languages, and theories of these different disciplines will converge, we will also begin to develop more common languages among them. This will also happen among people. We will talk further in later volumes about powerful hypertranslating applications that will come on the market in the next era, effectively removing the language barrier between people. We will also soon see more convergent forms of communicating emerge. These may be hieroglyphic- or symbol-based visual communication tools that accommodate different linguistic interpretations, or they may be common Internet languages that rapidly evolve in the same way that English has evolved from a hybrid of multiple different inputs and sources to facilitate international trade and communication. The Internet machine will itself accelerate this process in the Digitterran Tsunami, during which we will have a greater convergence of languages and cultures, to find a more easily widespread communication tool that we can all use.

Finally, and perhaps most controversially, the most poignant convergence is going to be between man and machine. We are going to be much more dependent on the Internet machine, and we are going to be more closely integrated with the Internet in our everyday lives. It will become more closely integrated with our physical persons through medical monitoring, autodiagnosing, and automedicating devices, and it will become more integrated with us culturally via our homes, cars, and portable wireless devices. As such we will see a greater convergence with the Internet in how we work, socialize, and live.

1.6   Codependence

The next Digitterran principle we will explore is codependence. In the Digitterran era, the idea of autonomy and separation is valid from some perspectives, but from others it is totally irrelevant. From one perspective, all things will be interconnected in a complex web of codependence, and there will be a high level of codependence among all things that exist in the whole system. For example, we will see a greater degree of codependence among data. In order for one piece of data to make sense, it will be dependent on many other bits of data. In order for it to have meaning and relevance, for it to fully exist, it will be dependent on the existence of other interrelated data. Similarly, systems will become much more codependent on each other. We can see, for example, that the GPS system, global satellite networks, and location-based telecommunications services are codependent. We spoke earlier about the convergence of different systems and about them being able to talk, co-relate, and share information with each other. As they do this more and more, they will become more codependent on each other. So Twitter, for example, will in ways become codependent on Facebook, as will Facebook become increasingly codependent on Twitter, as will Google become codependent on Facebook and Twitter as these systems reach their tipping point in wide-scale adoption. Also, the more these systems expand and become widely adopted, the more they will need to interoperate with other widely adopted systems and the more they will converge in the consumer space. This interoperability and convergence will start to draw all of the systems into a much more codependent and seamless ecosystem, because consumers will demand this and the systems will require it.

People also are going to become a lot more codependent on each other. We will all have increasingly self-centric demands of the internet, formed from our personal values, tastes, and interests, but our networks of friends we will also form a very important part of our self-centric framework and personal digital ecosystems. There will be a codependence between us and our network of friends, in terms of filtering content, making recommendations, keeping each other informed, and consuming information, as we will all be "touched" by what all others in our network are doing. So even though we will have a more self-centric perspective of the Internet in terms of our relationship with mass media publishers and commercial or political organizations, we will also have a greater codependence on each other in terms of being able to make sense of the highly fragmented and vast world of content in which we will find ourselves. In some ways, many people are going to experience a sort of information overload in the near future. Their networks will serve as important filter systems to help them discriminate between content that is of value and that which is not.

This principle will duplicate itself at the organizational level too. In order for organizations to be relevant to consumers, they are going to have to find creative ways of aligning themselves with other organizations so that they can deliver experiences to consumers that are more holistic, complex, and tacit to match the complexities of the different individuals and different kinds of profiles of consumers they are going to have to reach. Strategic alliances will enable them to deliver much more multifaceted experiences to consumers than they will be able to do autonomously, creating codependence between them, their strategic allies, and their increasingly diversified consumers.

Nations are also going to become a lot more codependent. We already do live in codependent multinational networks, but the degree of codependence is going to increase in the Digitterran era, not just in terms of sharing of resources but also in terms of defining and continuing our existence. Being that we will be entering a much more multipolar world with less monolithic lines of power and control, we can then see that codependency among nations and the way they operate will be amplified in the Digitterran era.

Perhaps the most radical of the codependence perspectives that we will need to appreciate in this environment, however, is the that which will emerge between the Internet itself and the community of man that it serves. There is going to become a much more symbiotic relationship between man and the Internet machine. We discussed this briefly before in the principle of convergence, citing the inevitable convergence of man and machine. This convergence will also drive a much greater degree of codependence between both.

We as people will become much more dependent on the Internet in order to be able to go about our daily lives, whether that be in driving our cars, finding our way to places, finding relevant information or entertainment that inspires and touches us, managing our diaries and lives, or staying in contact with our friends and family. We will depend on the web to schedule activities for us, to monitor our health, to manage our diets, and to manage our finances and our energy consumption. We will become much more dependent on the Internet machine to help us manage all of these things and be more effective and efficient in enjoying our lives.

Interestingly though, on the counterside, the machine too is going to become much more codependent on us. It's going to rely on us to teach it, to inform it, and provide it with information and development. One of the key challenges of the semantic web, for example, is the idea that machines don't understand language and information in the same way that humans do. It is going to need people to teach it that meaning through participation, interaction, and engagement.

It is going to be really important for the machine to have our perspective, our input into the system, in order for it to be able to improve itself, in order for it to be able to be more effective at doing what it needs to do and what we want it to do. We are not talking about a sentient machine at this stage. We are not talking about an advanced form of artificial intelligence either. But for the machine to be able to carry out even relatively simple functions, it will require greater relevance, greater focus, and better targeting capabilities. To achieve this, it will need us to provide it with a lot more input, with a lot more guidance, with a lot more data, with imagination, with vision, with perspective and morality—with all of the human things that are alien to the machine but that come to us naturally. So we can see a rich, bilateral codependence that will be necessary between the Internet and us for both us and the machine to be able to thrive as we go forward. It will be important for us to understand and appreciate this as we develop our systems, applications, and businesses.

1.7   Continuity

Another Digitterran principle that is important for us to understand is that of continuity. Continuity will occur in many areas of our lives in the Digitterran era. From a technological perspective, technologies that have been created in the past will continue to be present and reapplied in the next wave. There is an interesting video on YouTube with Kevin Kelly discussing the continuity of technology.[6] He has done research to show that every technology that we have ever created in human history exists and remains in production today. Every technology or tool that we find in antiquity can be found being replicated and produced in the world today. Steam engines, gramophones, cartridge decks, woodblock presses, quail pens, even Stone Age flint tools are being produced by people and being made available to the market somewhere on the planet today. Whatever the technology is, it continues to exist with us today. So when we talk of continuity in the context of technology, we mean the continued presence and use of previous technologies.

More relevant for us from a Digitterran perspective though will be the continuity of information and data. Old, legacy data that may have been stored in different places historically will become available and useful to us in the Digitterran era. Systems will be able to access data from legacy sources and utilize it in a

---

[6] www.youtube.com/watch?v=J132shgliuY&feature=related

continuous manner. We will be able to mine, reapply, and learn from old and new data and from combinations of both. An example of this kind of approach is the carbon dating of archaeological artifacts. Carbon dating allows us to extract information from ancient artifacts and use that data to develop knowledge with modern algorithms, theories, and applications. In similar ways, legacy systems and databases will provide us with data that will offer new insights into modern trends. As we have discussed, data will be a huge engine for innovation and creativity. The more data we can extract from both historic and current sources, the more information and knowledge we will be able to compile. As such, historic data will continue to be relevant and useful, as will new and future-focused data.

Also, in the physical realm, things themselves will be more continuous. In the pre-twenty-first-century world, manufacturers essentially produced goods and distributed them to retailers, who sold them to consumers. Consumers bought them, and that was effectively the end of the relationship, bar some sort of sparse after-sales services provided within warranty periods. In the Digitterran era, this is going to change significantly. There will be a much more continuous product life cycle and continuous relationship among manufacturers, products, and consumers, not only in terms of the servicing of products after sales but also in the origin of products in the first place. As people become more ecologically aware and socially active, they will become more concerned around how products come into being and that they come into existence in an ecologically balanced way. It will become commonplace for manufacturers to make public the full value chain for products, from the procurement of natural resources all the way through to the processes and facilities that are used to convert these resources into finished products. Customers will want to see that companies are operating in ecologically balanced and socially responsible ways. They will want to see that they have efficient and carbon-neutral logistic footprints and packaging processes and that they do not exploit children or disadvantaged communities. Internet technologies will enable companies to demonstrate this and customer interest groups to track it. Also, when it comes to disposing of products, the web will enable us to do so in socially responsible and ecologically balanced ways. We may, for example, want to see old electronic goods recycled and then entering the production cycle of new goods. We may wish to see old clothes recycled and going toward providing clothing for the homeless. The web will allow us to dictate and track such things, making our relationship with physical items much more continuous.

Additionally, once products are acquired, they will enable customers and producers to maintain continuous relationships with each other and with other buyers of the product. In this sense, relationship marketing will become a critical marketing skill and means of building loyalty with customers. This will be more easily facilitated by way of the fact that products themselves will be connected to the Internet in the Digitterran era.

So there will be this continuous relationship among a product, its manufacturer, and consumers. From a marketing perspective, manufacturers will use products as a means to build continuous relationships with consumers, retain them, and bring them into the fold for future products and future services. A product sold will be an opportunity to establish a relationship with a consumer, and the more continuous that relationship can be, the more profitable it will be for the company.

An example of what this might look like is if someone were to buy a stereo or an electronic piece of equipment in the Digitterran era, it will automatically bring the consumer into contact with a community of other users of that device. The buyer might be able to learn and share information with this community via some sort of social application interface with the product, enabling people to offer tips and advice on how to get the best out of the device. The device will also remain in touch with the factory so it can keep itself updated and maintained. It might also provide information to its owner of new services, supplies, or other products from the manufacturer that can be used in parallel or to enhance the product. It may entitle the user to acquire entertainment content from the manufacturer's network partners for free or at discounted prices.

Another important trend touched on above that we will see in the Digitterran era is the proliferation of evolving products. Consumers will no longer buy products that are static in their production cycles but will seek those that continue to evolve through software updates and application innovations.

This thinking is one of the great innovations of the Apple iPhone. Prior to the iPhone, most cell phones had limited life cycles and came with a set of features and applications that stayed the same throughout the life span of the phone. If customers wanted new features and applications on their phones, they essentially had to wait for a new model to be released with new functions, buy it, and dispose of their old one. Apple radically changed this model by separating the hardware of the phone from its software, just as one would do with a computer. It also had the brilliance to develop a user interface that was fluid and electronic, meaning it could change depending on what applications were running on the phone at the time. This separation between hardware and software, fluid user interface, and the creation of an open mart for application development is what made the iPhone truly revolutionary as a cell phone. It meant that a customer could buy an iPhone and the phone could continue to evolve and develop with new software updates and new applications, making the phone increasingly useful and new to consumers and expanding the cycle of its utility. Even now I am constantly discovering new features and applications for my iPhone, and there are over one hundred thousand applications available on the iTunes store for me to use to truly personalize my device to my needs. I believe this approach will expand to other product categories in the Digitterran era. I can envision evolving automobiles, televisions, stereos, furniture, cooking equipment, and even buildings. All will have a much greater continuity with their manufacturers, customers, and communities.

There will also be intelligence in digital-era items themselves, which will be able to do their own diagnostics and indicate when they require servicing or maintenance. In some cases they will even be able to automaintain and autoservice themselves via permanent connections to the Internet. We will see this, for example, in the automotive industry, with cars that will start to have a perpetual connection with the factory via the cloud. Digital-era cars will be able to diagnose themselves, identify when they need servicing, and suggest the best local service center to which to take the car. They will also be able schedule a service appointment that fits in with their owner's schedule, automatically.

On the consumer side, experiences will also be continuous in the digital era. Let us look at entertainment, for example, in the current landscape. Those who go to the cinema currently go to a movie theater and watch a film, and effectively the experience is concluded. Nowadays, if it is a real blockbuster success, it might generate a video game on the back of the film's success, but that is essentially it. At the front end there may be some engaging digital marketing assets produced before the film, but these generally are there to build the interest in the film, and once we have been to see it, the producers generally have no further use for us. More progressive companies might be keen to see that we say favorable things online about the film so others might go and see it, but that again is the end of the studio's interest in us once we have bought a ticket and seen the film. In the Digitterran era, this will not be the case. Actually, the whole cinematic experience itself is going to change in the Digitterran era, which we will discuss later in this series when we explore the impact of the Digitterran Tsunami on the entertainment element of the sociocultural spectrum.

From where we are now though, we can see the need for changes in the cinematic experience in the Digitterran era. The engagement of consumers prior to the completion of the film will start to increase. Digital media will be used in much more continuous ways to generate interest prior to a film, to sustain it during the film, and to continue it after seeing the film. The model of the future will be to retain some sort of continuity of that cinematic experience outside the cinema. It might be by way of taking personalized portable components of the experience away with one on a mobile device that can be shared on a social network. It might be a way of immersing oneself in the story somehow and sharing that with a community of fans of the film. The important thing though will be that the experience continues on.

We will see this also with people when they go on vacations and when they go to events. These might be the theater, concerts, or similar experiences. There will be this drive to have some sort of continuity of the experience. Experiences will become like centers of gravity that expand out virtually, geospatially, and temporally, i.e., they happen in a particular space in time, but the Internet will allow the experience to expand further beyond that space and time. For example, when U2 recently did a live stream on YouTube, that experience was in a particular space in time, and there were people who were at the Rose Bowl in Los Angeles who experienced it directly. The experience, however, was allowed to reverberate over the Internet, via YouTube, so other people could see it up to four days later. This is a very basic model of the idea. Much more intricate and sophisticated versions will emerge in the Digitterran era. We will start to see experiences expand from an epicenter or most concentrated part over a temporal dimension, as well as over a spatial dimension as experiences are amplified and interwoven with physical world and virtual world events. This is going to be a very powerful principle in the Digitterran era. It's going to enable a much richer degree of connectivity between experiences, a much richer level of immersion for people in how we socialize, and a much more continuous format of entertainment.

Finally, we will be more continuous ourselves. By way of our lifecasting and life caching culture, we will leave extensive footprints and archives of our lives behind even when we have passed on. Our descendants will be able to have much richer understandings of who we were, how we lived, and what we did than any generation before them. Our lives will therefore have a continuity to them that is unprecedented.

The Seven Social Principles

The second set of seven Digitterran principles outline the changes emerging in our societies driving the Internet's evolution.

1.8   Consumerization

Consumerization is where companies bring market-leading technologies to the consumer market ahead of business and industrial markets, achieving economies of scale and low pricing. As a result of consumerization, many of the major services and applications we use in our daily lives have become available to us through the web for free or very low prices. Though consumerization as a trend began in our Web 2.0 world, it will continue and gain significant momentum during Web 3.0. The research company Gartner says that consumerization will be the most significant trend affecting IT during the next ten years.[7] As

---

[7] http://www.gartner.com/press_releases/asset_138285_11.html

such, while consumerization was seeded in the Web 2.0 era, it will come into full bloom during the Digitterran era and is consequently included here as a key Digitterran principle.

Eventually many of the services we require will be available to us via the Internet for nominal fees or effectively for free. There will be models other than charging consumers for services, which will enable organizations to monetize providing such services. This is the consumerization model, a model we can see fully effective in our world today. One needs only to look at the incredible services offered to consumers by Google, Facebook, Myspace, Hotmail, Yahoo!, Twitter, and others to see this model in effect currently. The phenomenon has become so prolific that now one of the biggest problems facing Fortune 500 companies in the current climate is that their employees have a much richer, faster, and better Internet experience at home than they do when they are in the office. A decade ago corporations could provide better computers, better connection speeds, and larger data storage facilities to employees than most people had at home. Now the contrary is the case. Products and services have now been consumerized to the point that companies are struggling to keep up. This has been a major driver of the digital revolution. It has meant that the digital revolution has fundamentally become a consumer-led revolution as opposed to a business-driven one. This is a critical trend that must be grasped in order to appreciate how the web is evolving. Also, being that there are many more consumers in the marketplace than there are companies, and that there are much greater opportunities for economies of scale and thus commercial advantages for companies pursuing this route than the business-focused services route, the trend is unlikely to recede.

It is a huge problem for most companies today. Employees come into the office and they cannot access the websites that their agencies are developing for them, although they can easily view them at home. This is usually due to security restrictions, network-capacity issues, infrastructure, and storage-capacity problems on their office networks. A perfect example of this is e-mail. Most people in major blue chip corporations nowadays will find restrictions on the e-mails that they can have, such as how long they can keep them. They will find they have to empty their e-mail accounts on a monthly if not weekly or daily basis in order to avoid alarm messages from the IT department for having full mailboxes. In contrast, on their home computers and Gmail, Hotmail, or Yahoo! accounts, they have close to limitless capacity to receive, send, and store e-mails for a very small or no fee.

E-mail has been consumerized and provided by the aforementioned companies much more effectively than can be done by corporate organizations. This is a trend that is going to continue, so much so that progressive companies will be those that leverage these consumerized services as opposed to trying to ostracize or compete with them. Very few corporations will be able to develop an e-mail system as effective or secure as Google, Yahoo!, MSN, or Apple. They simply do not have the resources to commit to such an endeavor competitively. And the fallacy of security is exactly that. There is rarely more security behind most corporate firewalls than there is with the services of these providers. After all, secure facilities are part of the service offerings that are being consumerized.

Again, very few corporations in the world will be able to invest in the level of security for these services that companies that specialize in this area will be able to deliver to consumers, at least competitively. There are no non-technology-dedicated companies in the world that will be able to invest in a social networking infrastructure as rich, advanced, and sophisticated as Facebook, because that is Facebook's business, and it has consumerized that product and made it available to the masses for free. It has also invested in an infrastructure that can support the social networking needs of up to four hundred million people at last count. When one considers that Facebook provides large photography and video storage and sharing capabilities to all its users for free, one starts to get a sense of the scale of the consumerization phenomenon and how difficult it is for companies to keep pace with it using their current IT strategies.

This phenomenon of services becoming available online for free or at very low cost will continue. It will consume many of the current real-world services that we pay for. An example of this is telecommunications. Advanced telecom services will become consumerized in the next wave of the Internet. Our voices will simply become another form of content traveling over our ubiquitous, ever-present web. Skype has shown the viability of this by providing free Internet-to-Internet-based phone calls.

I believe a fundamental business principle of the Digitterran era is that all things that can easily be duplicated, provided, and reproduced virtually will trend toward zero cost to the consumer and things that are harder to duplicate electronically will command a premium. This, I believe, is a key concept for companies to understand in order to identify where they add value in their value chain and hence their business's reason for existence.

Consumerization will continue to drive huge changes in the relationship between corporations and people and between employers and employees, as well as where and how we interact with ourselves through the Internet. The leading applications and services that we require will be provided to us on a free or low-fee basis for the foreseeable future. This will lead to better and richer consumer experiences and a continually accelerating pace of change in the consumer landscape.

1.9   Multipolarity

Another major Digitterran principle is that of multipolarity. In the Digitterran era we are going to move away from simple mono-polar relationships across single dimensions to much more complex multipolar relationships across multiple dimensions.

At a consumer level, we are going to see that the demographic information of a person is not going to be able to define that consumer in the way that it has in previous eras. We are going to see a greater interplay among demographics, psychographics, cultural affiliations, and a multitude of different dimensions in defining a person. We will start to form much more complex models of how we categorize people. When we take the principle of granularity, the fact that people will have many different nodes of activity or reference points in their profiles, giving a multidimensional, complex halo to who they are, we start to see the principle of multipolarity taking its tone in terms of people's lives. Also, it will become quite normal for people to have various types of profiles. In the West we see this now where people might have a more serious and professional profile on LinkedIn versus a more casual and open profile on Facebook. In Asia this trend is much more profound. People tend to have professional profiles, social profiles, and alter ego profiles. Consumers in Japan and South Korea, for example, are more comfortable with fictional alter ego-like profiles in many of their social spaces than the "reality-anchored" ones popular in the West. Additionally, people have multiple profiles they use in gaming worlds, adding to the multitude of poles they have to their overall online presence.

Multipolarity is also going to become more apparent in the overall Internet culture. We are going to start to see a more multicultural and multilingual Internet. The idea of Anglo-American culture being the dominant or singular cultural pole of the web is going to change. We will start to see much greater diversity in the entertainment, information, and data content of the web as a whole. This is evidenced by the recent announcement by the Internet Corporation for Assigned Names and Numbers (ICANN), the body responsible for assigning Internet users their online addresses. ICANN revealed it will now allow the use of any of the world's scripts to create Internet address names. Up until this ruling, all Internet addresses had to be written in the Latin alphabet. ICANN President and CEO Rod Beckstrom described the ruling as a historic move toward the internationalization of the Internet. It will make the Internet more accessible to millions of people in Asia, the Middle East, and Russia. The US government also recently agreed to changes that will result in ICANN no longer solely reporting to the United States. We can thus see that the overriding structure and information architecture of the Internet is going to become much more multipolar.

Also, journalism and news distribution are going to become much more multipolar. We will start to see a lot more diversity in premium entertainment, as high-quality media production tools become much more consumerized and available to publishers in emerging markets. We will see a proliferation of content from many different parts of the world that will resonate with different interest groups in other parts of the world. This is going to create a much more multipolar, generic Internet culture, with much more diversity as well as more similarity and commonality.

In terms of the dimensions of the web, the Internet is also going to become a much more multidimensional medium. For example, it is going to become a much more four-dimensional space, whereby you will be able to identify things across four dimensions—the three classic geospatial dimensions of space with the additional dimension of time. You will be able to go into a room and understand what that room was yesterday, or what happened there yesterday, and extract media or "memories"— activities that happened yesterday or weeks, months, years, or decades before—from the room via mobile devices. Thus time will play an important role in how we experience the Internet and will become one of the key dimensions of the web. We will also start to form a much more four-dimensional perspective of our world, and we can expect a much more multidimensional Internet as we go forward.

Again, as previously mentioned, complex multidimensional personalities will become the norm, and organizations will start to recognize that people have multidimensional personalities formulated by different experiences, tastes, exposures, and interests. We will build up much more multipolar profiles of people and their networks than we do currently. This understanding of multiple interests and alliances will start to come to the fore in terms of how we understand people, organizations, and governments.

At the organizational level, this multipolarity and multidimensionality is going to play out in a very similar way to how it does at the individual level. Organizations will need to have more rounded and complex relationships with their customers, owing to the fragmentation and challenges they will face from the increasingly diversified and demanding customer range that they will need to service. Even the way in which companies exist online will change. In addition to opening web address to non-Latin characters, ICANN also recently announced it was liberalizing the market for domain name extensions, i.e., the .com or .co.uk part of a web address. This in theory means that anyone can now apply for a domain name extension. This means companies can set up domains for the group, for products, for markets, etc. For example, Sony might set up .sony, or usa.sony for the United States or europe.sony or vaio.sony, etc. So we can see that organizations will be able to operate in a much more multipolar manner in how they structure and present themselves online.

In meeting their social responsibility quotas and objectives, they are also going to have to develop much more multipolar and sometimes even diametrically opposed perspectives of their offerings. We can already see examples of this in several corporate social responsibility campaigns. The responsible-drinking campaigns of the alcohol beverage companies and the anti-smoking campaigns led by the tobacco companies are examples of these kinds of polarizations and complexities. Thus organizations too will become increasingly multidimensional and complicated in the Web 3.0 world.

Politically we are going to see a much more multipolar world. The emergence of the G20 group of nations as the leading international body to address global financial issues, replacing the previously Euro-centric G7 group, is perhaps the most stark demonstration of this. Multicultural perspectives and anchor points are going to be the norm in the next decade. We already see the emergence of Europe as a region with different political and commercial goals from North America. Newly elected Japanese Prime Minister Yukio Hatoyama has also brought to the fore the case for an East Asian Economic Community, which would integrate the economies of China, Japan, and other East Asian states. He has also called for a review of the fifty-year-old US-Japan Treaty of Mutual Cooperation and Security, highlighting the need for Japan, the world's second-largest economy, to have a more multipolar role with its neighbors and the world as a whole. China's emergence as an economic powerhouse that rivals the United States is inevitable and significant in China's role in a new multipolar world. Also, the emergence of the BRIC-M nations of Brazil, Russia, India, China, and Mexico as rapidly growing global economies highlights the important role these countries will play in the multipolar next decade.

1.10   Borderlessness

Borderlessness is another crucial Digitterran principle. It is not one that is necessarily new, but it is going to become ever more accentuated and prominent in the digital world. In the Digitterran era, content will be borderless, systems will be borderless, and networks will be borderless. The current restrictions around content will start to disappear, and the idea of a global community will become much more tangible and prevalent. The notion of restricting content, data, or communications to artificial borders will become less and less effective or important.

At the individual level, it means that people will connect with people wherever they are in the world as long as they have common interests and they can find each other, which the technology will enable them to do. Even within organizations, the idea of firm borders between them and other organizations will start to become redundant.

In order for collaboration and innovation to really flourish, there is going to be a need to dissolve the borders currently used to contain them. This is evident in the emergence of many of today's successful collaboration groups, including collaborative innovation networks, or CoINs as they are known. The most successful CoINs tend to emerge of their own need. They are formed by like-minded people coming together, across different networks and boundaries, whether those boundaries are geographic, cultural, organizational, academic, or whatever. These people come together based on the commonality of the interests of the individuals and their shared goal of solving a problem or resolving a need. The thing that pulls people together and which causes people to gravitate around causes is the level of interest for the subject that is at the center of that grouping, not the boundaries around the people in the group. The boundaries become increasingly meaningless; it is the people who are drawn to the central principle who are pulled into such groups. Organizations that recognize and encourage this will thrive.

Some restrictions will persist, and some groups will continue to restrict themselves or elements of their collaborations, but those by default will not be the ones that enable the greatest degree of innovation. Furthermore, most of the filters that persist will not be ones based on current borders. They will be based on the complexity of the characters that are forming and the common ground between the complex character profiles of the group's members, rather than on externalized borders that are simply representations of geographic, geopolitical, or commercial constraints. This is not to say that all organizational borders will disappear. What is more likely to happen is that they will increasingly blur and become more fluid and less permanent, i.e., borders may have to be erected around information and data, but this will happen more when the data necessitates it, such as in cases with legislative or privacy protection concerns. Additionally, more granular and dynamically configurable information-protecting systems will emerge, enabling borders to rise and fall as needed around the sensitivities of information being shared as opposed to being more permanently established around organizational restraints as they are currently.

1.11   NEO-Tribalism

The next Digitterran principle is NEO-tribalism. Tribalism is a bit of a precarious term, because it has come to mean many things over the ages. We are all at least somewhat familiar with the traditional meaning of the word *tribe* or the traditional concept of a tribe, i.e., a group or clan of people who are related by some sort of genetic family or extended clan line that brings them together, sharing a common culture, environment, language, etc.

However, we are referring to a new neo-tribalism here, not the classic tribal model. Neo-tribalism in itself is also something of a precarious term, because it also has many different interpretations. For the purpose of this work, we will define neo-tribalism as new earth order (hence, NEO) tribalism. This tribalism refers to people coming together in communities or tribes that are centered on ideas, common interests, experiences, or goals. Critically, these interests need not be defined by geography, genetics, family, clan, nation, or any kind of externally imposed commonality. NEO-tribes are simply tribes that form around shared beliefs, ideas, interests, or pursuits. They are at the heart of a new social order that the Digitterran Tsunami will bring, and they represent a significant social evolutionary leap enabled by the Internet.

One important thing to understand is that NEO-tribalism can occur on multiple dimensions. People can be members of many different tribes catering to different interests. For example, people might be members of professional tribes, or they might be members of religious tribes. They might also be members of social tribes while they are members of community tribes while remaining members of sporting tribes. All the fans of a particular football club, such as the Arsenal or the Washington Redskins, or of the Ferrari or McLaren Formula One teams, wherever they are in the world, are all part of a tribe. These represent a community of people who share a common interest and a common goal, i.e., winning the Premier League, the Super Bowl, or the Formula One Championship. Some people may be more active tribe members than others, and some might have more power or privileges within the tribe than others—and such power and privilege can act as a strong magnet to attract or repel potential new tribe recruits. Tribes may have colors, languages, symbols, codes, and behaviors expected of members. Sporting tribes are a very good example of how diverse and spread tribes can be. Again, in professional environments people will also join tribes that might call for different behaviors, cultures, and language. The key point though is that people will be members of many different tribes, and the things that drive them into these tribes will be multifaceted. Many interesting theories have emerged around the whole concept of tribes, and tribalism is a multidimensional phenomenon in our modern world. Many writers argue that we have remained a very tribal species from our earliest civilizations and earliest cultures and that we have a tribal nature at the hearts of our social and human nature.

I want to explore the notion that the way we organize our societies has morphed and changed over the millennia and, as I have said, that the Internet and social media represent a social evolutionary turning point for our planet and species.

History shows us that to date there have been three major kinds of social organization models. One is the early tribal model, where people were born into a clan or into a community and they grouped together to gather and hunt food in a particular area of land. The tribe effectively shared genetics, language, culture, and customs. Most members were from common family lines, usually forming a cluster of clans in a small community. A group with a few hundred people would constitute a tribe in this sense, though these tribes could grow considerably in numbers over the ages.

History tells us the next social organizational model was that of kingdoms and empires. Effectively, when kingdoms were formed, kings brought together a strong martial force and a stronger financial capability than any local tribe and basically conquered all tribes previously in the area, bringing them into their supertribe or kingdom. Kingdoms by the same mechanic expanded across regions into empires, becoming stronger and more powerful as they expanded and consumed more tribes and kingdoms along their way. In notable cases, these kingdoms became empires that sometimes expanded across multiple regions and large parts of the globe. The Egyptian, Ghanaian, Benin, Greek, Roman, Chinese, Persian, Portuguese, Spanish, and even British empires exemplify such pan-regional and eventually pan-global fiefdoms.

The kingdom and empire model reigned supreme and effectively until it became superseded by the national republic model. The term *republic* is believed to originate from Italian Renaissance writers, most notably Niccolo Machiavelli, who described two forms of government: principalities ruled by a monarch and republics ruled by the people. The republican movement was formed in medieval Italy by a wealthy mercantile class that found itself increasingly powerless in the feudal system of Italy. The Holy Roman Empire, loosely governed by the Vatican, agreed to grant free imperial city status to fifty-one of the largest city-towns in Italy. These became free city-states, many of which were under the control of merchant councils. These states opted to form "republican" governments elected by the people, though the city-states still fell under the ultimate jurisdiction of the Roman Emperor. At this time republican thinking and philosophy focused on governments being appointed and serving the needs of citizens spread widely across Europe. It was, however, generally accepted as being a form of government that could thrive with small city-state-like communities. It was with the French Revolution and the birth of the First French Republic that republics became contenders in political culture as viable ways of governing large nations. With the American Revolution and the formation of the United States in 1781, the idea became consummated, and republics replaced monarchist rule the world over. Today only a handful of true monarchist kingdom governments remain.[8] Once the republic model came into being, the kingdom and empire model was superseded and could not survive in its previous guise much longer, as can be seen in our modern world.

The United Kingdom is a very good example of a country that has gone through this complete transition. Prior to the Roman invasion of Britain in 43 CE, various kings and houses often at war and overthrowing one another ruled Britain. It was essentially a tribal nation. The Kingdom of England was formed from a heptarch of seven small Anglo-Saxon kingdoms of south, east, and central Britain in the Dark Ages, the period following the Roman departure from Britain around 500 CE. This kingdom joined the kingdoms of Scotland and Wales in 1707 to form the United Kingdom of Great Britain, with a centralized monarch and crown residing in London. It was from this seat that the global British Empire was established and controlled. However, from the English Civil Wars of 1640 onward, the crown gradually lost more and more power to the parliament of the people till it effectively became the republic it is today. Even though it still remains a kingdom technically and in name, the power of parliament has ascended considerably over the years and the power of the crown receded to what are now theoretical and rarely used *reserve powers*. The republic nation model has superseded the kingdom and empire model in all but name and ceremony.

[8] Interestingly, prior to the European global colonial era there were a sum total of fourteen nations in the world. Now there are 195.

What all these models—tribes, kingdoms, empires, nations, and republics—share is that they fundamentally have been anchored to land. In the tribal model, tribes were groups of people who came from a particular area and who lived together and formed a society in a physical space. Kingdoms became an extension of that rule over land. Nations became extensions of these kingdoms, still very much anchored to the land on which the previous tribes and kingdoms were centered, ignoring migration patterns. So you could not have a nation, for example, that wasn't anchored to a piece of land on a particular longitude and latitude of the planet. International law has no current provision for a sovereign state with no physical borders or land mass.

We are now, however, entering a new era with a new model of social organization emerging. We do not really have a name for it yet, which is a problem. So, for the purpose of convenience, I'm calling it NEO-tribalism. NEO-tribes are more granular than nations but are not the same as traditional tribes. The primary difference between NEO-tribes and classic models of tribes, kingdoms, and nations is that NEO-tribes are not anchored to physical spaces. A name that has been proposed for this social unit is phyles, based on the Greek word for clanlike groupings that might be separated by space but were joined by ideas. There were twelve phyles in ancient Greece and Athena that formed the counties and nations of Athena. These phyles effectively constituted common groups that might include companies, tribes, families, clans, etc. They were akin to fraternities or communal groups based around similar interests and goals. The common interests and ideas were more important than geographic proximity with phyles. NEO-tribes share this trait with phyles.

Since they are built around ideas and beliefs rather than bloodlines or land, they represent a new social unit and hence a new way of socially organizing ourselves. I have named these new units New Earth Order Tribes to articulate the point. The important point though is not what we call these new units but that a new social unit is emerging.

NEO-tribes are a significant turning point in the social anthropological evolution of our planet in that for the first time people can now easily group together and interact regularly regardless of where they are in the world, based on common interests and beliefs alone. This principle is colossal in scope from the social, cultural, and political perspective of the Digitterran Tsunami.

This social unit will enable people to group together in solid communities based around ideas and common interests rather than around geographic proximity or national boundaries. Based on the dynamics of global citizenship, globalization, regionalism and planetarianism, these groups are likely to become so relevant, meaningful, and powerful to the people of the world that they will supersede the nation model and enable people to live in new and more fluid social-political structures.

The dynamics of these NEO-tribes will be multifaceted and have many elements to them. They will also have many levels. Seth Godin, famous author and speaker on new trends, describes NEO-tribes as change driven by correct leadership. He says that ideas plus tribes equal movements. He says an important factor with NEO-tribes, versus nations and our current cultural models, is that large numbers and massive audiences do not drive their growth.

They are more about quality than quantity. NEO-tribes seek the true believers of the ideas that lead to their formation, not the biggest number of followers. This in effect makes them epicenters or centers of gravity for ideas and concepts. When they find the true believers of their ideas, they can then start a movement. That movement can be global in scope and huge in terms of its impact, but that is not what drives it. What drives it is a qualitative necessity to connect with like-minded people. It is a true belief in particular ideas and goals about which people are passionate that is the essence of what these NEO-tribes are about. Though these groupings may occur, as I have said, across work, social, political, or multiple other dimensions, they become effective in driving change primarily based on the ability of the core ideas to connect with other people who are passionate about the ideas espoused and those people taking action to get momentum behind the tribe's goals.

1.12   Planetarianism

Planetarianism is the term I have coined to define a new grass-root, planetwide social awareness. It is an awareness of the people of the planet about themselves, about their communities and other communities, about other people on the planet, about the planet itself, about the social and ecological credentials of the organizations and companies of the world, and about the interconnectedness and interrelationship among them all.

It differs from Kenichi Ohmae's globalism. Globalism has come to represent the globalized operations of multinational companies, large corporations, and nation-states and how they leverage their operations and resources to maximize their profits and revenues across the globe. Politically, globalism has come to represent a trend toward the integration of national states into a centralized and pan-global governance system centered on the principles of freedom of movement of goods and the freedom of trade. Globalism has many advocates and critics and is the center of a heated debate between opposing camps, resulting in demonstrations around the planet and much political and commercial maneuvering within companies and governments. Overall it is safe to say, however, that globalism is very much associated with the activities of multinational businesses, international governance organizations, and nation-states.

Planetarianism, on the other hand, is a more grassroots perspective on the globalization phenomenon. It is more about people of the planet connecting with other people in different parts of the planet. It is about people of the planet being aware of the planet, being aware of themselves as citizens of the planet, and about them being protective of the planet and each other in terms of how they go about their lives and what they demand of themselves, from their leaders, and from the enterprises of the world. Planetarianism is more of a grassroots people movement than globalism, which is more of a top-down multinational corporation and government movement. Planetarianism is fundamentally about communities and networks of people connecting with other networks of people. It is a proactive, socially progressive movement facilitated by a planetwide web of interconnected, socially networked NEO-citizens.

In this context it is always important to remember that as human beings, we are extremely social creatures. It is a key need for of us as human beings to socialize, engage, and interact with other human beings. We also need to be accepted by other people. These needs for social connectedness and interconnectedness are important drivers for the planetary movement, for they provide a foundation for understanding why we will join networks and organizations seeking to highlight and change social issues.

However, the counterside of this, as we will shortly explore, is that people will become much more granular in their needs and desires and they will be much more comfortable with being unique as individuals in comparison with the people who immediately surround them. What the web will give people, is a means to maintain a social interconnectedness with like-minded people who may not necessarily be in the same part of the world. This will enable people to fulfil their needs, to interact and be accepted, while at the same time exploring themselves in more profound ways and expressing their uniqueness. As such, people's networks of friends and influencers will become much more international and transregional. Consequently the information and entertainment they consume will become much more international and transregional, as we discussed with the principle of interconnectedness. Therefore their interests and current affairs reference points will also inevitably become much more international and transregional. Planetarianism defines the awareness created by this new social neural network and the resultant social activism it inspires and precipitates around the world.

The Internet provides the infrastructure through which people can connect with other people around the world and through which they can become aware of issues that are affecting other people to which they themselves may be sympathetic. These might be human rights issues, ecological issues, or animal rights issues, for example. They may be entertainment, cultural, academic, or political issues. The important thing is that they will be issues that are important to the person in question and things that are important to other people in their network. That shared sense of importance around the issue will bond these people and resonate through their virtual communities, driving them to differing degrees of unified action regardless of their geographic dispersion. The Internet will also provide them with the tools and means to take effective action easily. This is the principle of planetarianism. Planetarianism is going to be a movement within which people will start to understand themselves and operate, think, communicate, and connect with other people in a planetwide context, based on their shared interests, as opposed to being based on their geographic locations or cultural heritage.

Also, as I say, one of the key drivers of the planetary movement and the planetary perspective will be ecological awareness. People will become much more proactive in championing ecological rights and ecological responsibility from corporations and governments. Planetarianism will emphasize the need that people have to protect the environment that sustains qualitative human life. Ecological awareness and ecological sensitivity will be pillars of planetarianism, as will human rights and social responsibility sensitivities. Via planetarianism there will also be a sort of planetwide drive for learning, culture exchange, social activism, and civil rights protection of all people of the world. We can already see traces of this starting to happen, and governments are going to have to be much more sensitive to external influences from people in different parts of the world in how they operate in the political space.

1.13   Global Citizenship

Another crucial social-political principle of the Digitterran movement is the principle of global citizenship. Global citizenship will take the momentum, dynamic, and energy of the planetarianism movement and consolidate it in more structured and tangible rights of the people of the world, establishing a global platform for human rights.

Global citizenship is effectively a movement to globalize citizenship rights. This principle was established with the United Nations' adoption of the Universal Declaration of Human Rights in 1948, but it is going to gain considerable increased momentum in the Digitterran era. People will start to see themselves much more in the context of global citizens as opposed to simply national citizens. This will be in terms of their work rights, their human rights, their civil rights, and their freedom-of-speech rights. This is going to become increasingly important and is going to represent a real challenge for many governments of the world in how they organize, manage, and control their nationals.

We will explore some of the impacts of this when we discuss in future volumes the social-political climate that's coming within the Digitterran era. For now, suffice to say global citizenship is a principle that we are definitely going to see a greater amount of interest in during the Digitterran era. Most people, if not all people, will effectively have a dual citizenship: a citizenship of the country in which they reside, for which they will have national citizenship rights, and a citizenship of the world, for which they will have global citizenship rights. The Universal Bill of Human Rights will become recognized as de facto global citizenship rights. I believe that the Internet enables many articles of the Universal Bill of Human Rights to be made more tangible and enforceable in the Digitterran era. As a result, I believe we will see the emergence of some sort of Universal Bill of Digital Rights that augments the Bill of Human Rights and enables some human rights, such as freedom of speech and freedom of expression, to be digitally enforced and enabled.

The idea of all people, wherever they are in the world, having a base level of global digital rights will become much more pervasive, dynamic, and prevalent. This will drive political and social change to the extent that such a bill will eventually become ratified by the United Nations or some other supranational entity. Nations of the world will have to sign up to this bill. They will do this because their citizens will demand it of them. This global digital rights bill will be high level enough to allow countries to still retain sovereign decision rights on Internet usage within their nations while mandating the recognition in international law of some basic form of digital rights for all people of the planet so we can interact digitally at a basic level as one people.

I think one area where this could play out increasingly is in the energy sector. The idea of basic individual resource rights, global consumption rights, and planetwide intracitizen trading rights will start to take shape in the Digitterran era. People will be able to trade resource credits or resource rights they have with other citizens, and mechanisms facilitating such trade will emerge as part of the Digitterran Tsunami.

Picking up again on some of the things we have discussed previously, when we look at data-centricity and the impact that it will have in terms of us being able to manage our resources as a people, species, and global community, we can see our awareness will need to become much more holistic and interrelated. Rights will need to be developed and articulated that can provide a global baseline with which all of us can operate as interconnected individuals, nations, and organizations in a way that is harmonious, balanced, and sustainable. Global citizenship will be a cornerstone of this system.

1.14   Social Activism

Another principle that we will see rise, which also builds on the principles of planetarianism and global citizenship, is that of social activism.

In the Digital age, people will become much more engaged in social activism. This will happen for a number of reasons. First of all, it will become easier for people to mobilize and become active around a cause. Howard Dean's 2004 US Democratic presidential campaign's use of social networking sites Meetup.com and Moveon.org potently demonstrated this point in showing how easily people could be mobilized via the Internet. People will also be able to participate or contribute to a cause very easily without necessarily having to devote a great deal of time, resources, or effort. Barrack Obama's 2008 US presidential campaign also demonstrated this. The barriers toward people becoming socially active have come down considerably as a result of Web 2.0 technologies. Web 3.0 will make it even easier for people to become active socially. There is a cultural shift happening, and it will become much hipper for people to be socially active and to have a socially philanthropic element to their profile. It will become normal for people to be active in a cause or to support a cause as part of their consumption patterns or routines. They will promote these causes in their networks and make them part of their lives to have some sort of means of being able to verify and vindicate that they have contributed to causes that make the world a better place. This will become increasingly important to people in the Digitterran era.

This is also going to be amplified by the need of organizations and companies to promote themselves as good corporate citizens through social causes and social responsibility programs. They are going to need to generate social currency and social equity in the communities in which they operate and show that they are positively contributing to society. In order to activate and mobilize these social causes, they will need to get people to participate. There is thus a symbiotic relationship among organizations, people, and communities emerging here in getting under the skin of issues and trying to create social changes for the mutual benefit of consumers, commercial organizations, and communities within our societies that need help.

Another factor that's going to drive this phenomenon further yet is how easy it will be to track the progress of social causes people are helping. People in the nineteenth and twentieth centuries, and even earlier, supported social causes. But historically there has been less immediate and visible evidence of the impact of their contributions to such causes. When people give to Oxfam, Save the Children, or one of the myriad of other philanthropic organizations, the gap between giving and seeing evidence of that largesse having an impact on the community has been huge. This is going to be dramatically reduced in the Digitterran era. It will be much easier for people to see the results of their support for causes they have helped. This will catalyze people to do more and to contribute further. As we saw in previous examples involving the living data principle, what gets measured gets done. This notion will again play out in the field of social activism. The more that people can see that they are making differences in the world, the more they will be inspired to make more differences.

The final element of this principle is that people will feel more empowered by their activism. They are awakening by the day to the increased power they have as consumers. As we have shown, people are becoming aware that they are able to dictate what corporations do with some of their resources. There is a fantastic example of this in a recent campaign that Target carried out in the United States. The retailer had a roster of social causes it wanted to support. Rather than simply determining internally which of these causes it should sponsor, the company used Facebook to ask customers to vote on causes that should be funded. Customers therefore got to decide where the money went. This meant that Target was supporting causes that were important to its customers. It also implicitly meant that it was earning valuable social equity (and, dare I say, free advertising) with its customers by way of supporting causes that were truly important to them. It also meant that organizations consumers cared about were getting support from Target. This was a win-win situation for all and was a great example of how enterprises and consumers can easily work together to be active on social causes.

The social activism principle will be amplified and will increase substantially in the Digitterran era. It will be easier for people to be social activists. They will have a greater sense of empowerment and potential to effect change, and being able to track and see the influence that their activism has on the causes they support will encourage them to do more. Those trends, combined with the dynamics of planetarianism and global citizenship, will coalesce to drive a greater level of social activism around the planet.

Seven Ethical & Philosophical Principles

The final seven principles of the Digitterran Tsunami outline the ethical and philosophical issues that will drive the Internet's evolution.

1.15   Me-Centricity

A principle that is becoming increasingly important in the digital era is that of self-centricity or "me-centricity," as I am calling it. This principle talks to how the NEO-citizens and people of the next wave are going to be much more comfortable and confident with demanding experiences that are truly tailored and personalized to them. Understanding this will be crucial for the success of organizations that wish to reach and communicate with people in this era.

There is going to be a high degree of personalization, whereby content that is delivered from any media supplier or content publisher will need to be tailored and, in many circumstances, actually generated according to multiple different user profiles, types, and structures. The more tailored and targeted content is to each unique individual user, the more it will resonate with that user and the more that user will promote it within that person's community. The idea of resonance is a critical one in establishing a fit between content and users in the Digitterran era. It is typified in the principle of me-centricity. In order for content to truly resonate with me, it will have to be aligned with multiple aspects of me. This brings us back to the importance of data about me and of developing a rich and profound understanding of my universe, in order for companies to succeed in resonating their products and services with me.

The model of the me-centric Internet is very much the vision on which Facebook has been founded, and it forms the vision of how Facebook sees the Internet evolving in the future. Much has been written recently on the battle for domination of the Internet between the Google and Facebook camps. Google has had the vision of digitizing the world and delivering services to its citizens that are tailored to their needs and desires that it is able to deduce from the vast quantities of data it aims to aggregate on them. Certainly, the model of the Facebook camp is that everyone will effectively have his or her own personal Internet. They will have their own social filter through which they view the Internet, through which all content comes to them, and which prevents undesirable content from penetrating their personal web spaces. These filters, however, will enable them to discover content and services they may not have discovered via referrals and social sharing with their network of family, friends, and associates. This will effectively be an information and content-pulling system bringing content to them via their preferences and network of people. People will have personal firewalls through which no content will pass if they do not allow it. They will also have the firewalls of their network of peers, friends, family, and associates, who will again provide another rich filtering process. This will be both a filtering and sharing system and is likely to become a very effective way for people to manage the huge volume of content that will be available to them.

This model is an extremely relevant one that we will see much more of in the Web 3.0 world. The fact that people are going to have a greater sense of empowerment, a greater degree of comfort with their uniqueness and idiosyncrasies, and that they are going to have a greater belief in themselves, in their tastes and interests, will lead this trend and significantly shape their social profiles. This, coupled with them being able to find like-minded people with similar interests and profiles from other parts of the ecosystem with relative ease, also means this trend is likely to have far-reaching social and cultural implications. There is likely to be a much greater need for people to feel they are able to fully express themselves in the Digitterran era than a need to fit in with the people immediately around them. We are going to see a much greater degree of introspection in that sense. This will partly be driven by the living data principle we have discussed as people analyze the data they accumulate on themselves and their lives. There will also be a much greater degree of introspection, coming from people trying to really understand who they are, what motivates them, what excites them, and what they are about. The brand of "me" will become an increasingly important consideration to us all. Our networks of friends, family, colleagues, and associates will become much more transparent and interconnected, and as such the values and principles that we live by will become more important to us. There was an interesting scenario at the turn of the century, when the actor Leonardo DiCaprio registered his name as a trademark. I believe this is going to be a principle of the Digitterran era, when people will become as concerned with their own personal branding, endorsements, and associations as corporations are. People will become more focused on the interrelationship among these aspects in the Digitterran era, as they will become more focused on what they want out of life, society, and the world as a whole.

So we are going to have more self-centric Internet experiences and a greater degree of personal brand building as the trend for mass fame or "celeb-reality" that begun with the explosion of reality TV continues to rise. All of these things will coalesce to form very potent forms of personalized expressions of who we are and how we interact with others. This self-expression will continue in terms of what we consume and the companies and brands that we endorse. Companies that understand and embrace this degree of granular individuality, this granular uniqueness and me-centricity, will be much more successful than those that do not. People are going to feel much more comfortable in celebrating their uniqueness and finding like-minded people who share similar values on things that are important to them in their lives than conforming with those with whom they do not necessarily relate simply because they are in their proximity. The machine will enable us all to find like-minded people and establish meaningful bonds with them that resonate with and amplify our values and interests in ways previously unprecedented, further amplifying this trend.

1.16   Co-ownership

A major principle of the Web 2.0 movement has been that of collaboration and codevelopment. The use of wikis, blogs, forums, and social networks to create collaborative tools has been dramatic in the opportunities it has created. Resources such as Wikipedia all the way through to organizations that have developed themselves around the idea of collaboration and sharing demonstrate the power of this trend. A great book that delves into the detail of this is *Wikinomics (2007)* by Don Tapscott and Anthony Williams. It talks of the power of this collaborative way of thinking and some of the fruits that can be yielded from it. It demonstrates that new models of production and organization are emerging around community, collaboration, and self-organization rather than hierarchy and control. Collaboration has been a key dynamic of the whole Web 2.0 movement. Research shows that the most effective collaboration networks are those that emerge around people with a common need to solve a problem or to address an issue. These networks are increasingly forming across organizational borders, sometimes across competing organizational borders, across national, cultural, and even theoretical boundaries. Companies and organizations are starting to come to terms with this new way of thinking.

Additionally, consumers are becoming increasingly involved in creating campaigns, products, and ideas. Services and products are now developed across commercial boundaries, across disciplines, across national boundaries, etc. This is creating a new paradigm in innovation and creativity. It is also creating a new paradigm for intellectual property ownership. The pre-twenty-first-century model for IP was one of centralized ownership where IP was developed by a small group within an organization or by a single or small group of inventors. In the Web 2.0 world, the creative process has been distributed across networks. As such, the need for a distributed IP ownership model to replace the current centralized one is emerging. At the extreme end of this spectrum is the open source movement. The open source movement has moved software development from centralized IP ownership to a model of little or no IP ownership. This has driven a great amount of innovation on the web by enabling people across the planet to develop applications and services that can be consumed by other developers and the public without any licensing costs or fees. We are definitely going to see an expansion of the open source movement in the Digitterran era. It will expand beyond the software industry to the wider world. I believe we are going to see open source physical products and services in a much wider context permeate our world. I believe open source automotive platforms and consumer electronic platforms will be among the first of these new open source platforms we will see.

While the open source movement drives many great advantages in the proliferation of technology, products, and services, it also poses certain challenges. These can include reliability, stability, and support. Though these are becoming less problematic as the open source community expands and the mass of people reviewing, scrutinizing, and developing applications increases, they still remain as challenges to full proliferation of true open source products. As such it is likely that products will often be based on an open source core that is then refined and developed further by a company. An example of this would be Red Hat Linux, a refined and supported version of the Linux open source operating system provided by Red Hat. Mozilla's Firefox browser is another "refined" Linux-based application. The point here is that even with a full open source movement, there will still be a need for branded products that are refined and developed by companies from an open source core to stable and supported products. This will contribute to the trend of distributed and open IP ownership models for such products.

Another trend for which we have seen great uptake within the Web 2.0 world is that of user participation. This is taking the form of user-generated content such as blogs, mashups, cocreated videos, chat posts, etc. We are seeing user-generated marketing campaigns emerge and user-generated products and services, in terms of crowdsourced thoughts and ideas, across collaboration networks. We can thus see that we now have many touch points through which users are contributing toward the intellectual property of a company. As such, the ownership model for organizations' IP will need to change to reflect this. This is the rationale behind the Digitterran principle of co-ownership. Since users and people from other organizations are participating so much in the creation of product services, campaigns, etc., then effectively there is going to have to be a sharing of the ownership of the benefits generated by these assets. Whether that sharing is remunerated through social currency or through direct monetary payment to collaborators is yet is to be determined, and I am sure there will be many creative variations. But it is going to be important for companies to acknowledge the co-ownership of things that are created in this collaborative way and to open resulting IP so that it can be utilized, explored, and exploited in a much more open and shared way than would have been the case in the twentieth century.

Another important factor will be that a culture of contribution and sharing will become increasingly prevalent in the next wave. As such, in order for companies to retain positive profiles within their industries, they will be expected to make IP contributions or donations that progress the state-of-the-art in their industries. That is to say they will be expected to provide IP that is shared or co-owned by a wider community or the industry as a whole. We are already starting to see instances of this emerge. IBM, for example, has developed numerous patents it is making available to the IT industry as a whole, for the industry to develop, exploit, and utilize further.

I think there will be many more examples of this kind of hybridized approach to IP ownership.

There will, needless to say, still be intellectual property that is of significant competitive advantage that needs to be protected and retained by organizations in some way, but they will need to find a more open and communal way of protecting and sharing noncore and to some extent even core IP. This will be essential with collaborative networks like the wiki-driven collaborations we discussed earlier, because effective collaboration will start to happen in a much more borderless way. It is important to reiterate that open, borderless collaborations will lead to the biggest breakthroughs in innovation, so it is not something that most organizations will be able to opt out of and remain competitive.

1.17   Transparency

Another important trend we will see rise in the Digitterran era is transparency. The activities of individuals, organizations, and governments will become increasingly transparent and visible in the Digitterran era. It is going to become increasingly important for companies and governments to be as open as possible with consumers and citizens. It will be more difficult to keep things hidden in a digitally connected world than it has been in the analog one. This, coupled with the fact that it will be quite easy for any concerned consumer or citizen to broadcast any disingenuous or misleading activities carried out by organizations or governments to their network and a global audience, will drive a greater need for organizations to be transparent and honest with their customers on their activities. Most important, however, governments and organizations will start to see the benefits of opening up information and datasets to the public in enabling greater innovation and the creation of new services. We can already see this trend in motion in many parts of the world. In US President Obama's Open Government Initiative and Data.gov policy are clear vindications of this trend. The following is stated on the United States' Data.gov website:

> *The purpose of Data.gov is to increase public access to high value, machine readable datasets generated by the Executive Branch of the Federal Government.*

As a priority Open Government Initiative for President Obama's administration, Data.gov increases the ability of the public to easily find, download, and use datasets that are generated and held by the Federal Government. Data.gov provides descriptions of the Federal datasets (metadata), information about how to access the datasets, and tools that leverage government datasets. The data catalogs will continue to grow as datasets are added.

Public participation and collaboration will be one of the keys to the success of Data.gov. Data.gov enables the public to participate in government by providing downloadable Federal datasets to build applications, conduct analyses, and perform research. Data.gov will continue to improve based on feedback, comments, and recommendations from the public and therefore we encourage individuals to suggest datasets they'd like to see, rate and comment on current datasets, and suggest ways to improve the site.

A primary goal of Data.gov is to improve access to Federal data and expand creative use of those data beyond the walls of government by encouraging innovative ideas (e.g., web applications). Data.gov strives to make government more transparent and is committed to creating an unprecedented level of openness in Government. The openness derived from Data.gov will strengthen our Nation's democracy and promote efficiency and effectiveness in Government.

This open government and open data approach is now spreading around the United States, with the National Association of State Chief Information Officers (NASCIO) advocating that state governments also create public data catalogs, modeling the same open data approach of the national Data.gov. The American Lung Association used the Environmental Protection Agency's Air Quality System database to create a "State of the Air" report, an important assessment of environmental quality with ramifications especially for those with respiratory diseases such as asthma or emphysema. "Six out of ten people (61.7%) in the United States population live in counties that have unhealthy levels of either ozone or particle pollution," the report found. This is a prime example of how government data became a valuable public resource with a use out of the scope of the government agency that created it.

In Europe, the commercial value of public data when it is open as in the United States, as opposed to when it is closed as has been the case in most of Europe to date, is the subject of much debate. In the United States, open and unrestricted access to information has resulted in the rapid growth of information-intensive industries. That open government data is a boon to a national economy is supported by an NWS report (Weiss 2002) that compared the relative openness of data in the United States to the more prominent cost-recovery and licensing model in Europe, in which the public must generally purchase government data at a price much greater than the cost to distribute the information, and after which the purchaser may not legally redistribute it. The marginal cost of distribution is the cost of making one more copy. In the physical world, this is the cost of paper and postage. In the online world, it is the cost of transferring data over the Internet, which is so low as to make the marginal cost of distributing most government records essentially zero. The report noted that the weather risk management industry is fifty times larger in the United States than in Europe, attributable in part to the higher commercial value of weather data made available at marginal cost and without licensing restrictions in the United States compared with European nations, where weather data is expensive and more tightly controlled. The report indicates that open government data may even be more financially lucrative to government programs than cost recovery, as more applications built on open data can also translate into higher corporate taxes for the government. The report concludes, "Charging marginal cost of dissemination for public sector information will lead to optimal economic growth in society and will far outweigh the immediate perceived benefits of aggressive cost recovery."

The United Kingdom's Guardian newspaper's "Free our data" campaign is attempting to make data available to people by fighting closed data policies. The campaign proposes that making data available for use for free would vastly expand the range of services available to people. Research commissioned by the European Commission in a paper entitled "Commercial Exploitation of Europe's Public Sector Information" supports the idea. It suggests that the EU market would not have to even double in size for governments to easily recoup in extra tax revenues what they would lose by ceasing to charge for public sector information. A working group report to the Office of

Science Technology Policy, Executive Office of the President of the United States titled, "Harnessing the Power of Digital Data for Science and Society," describes the issue well: "The power of digital information to catalyze progress is limited only by the power of the human mind. Data are not consumed by the ideas and innovations they spark, but are an endless fuel for creativity. A small bit of information, well found, can drive a giant leap of creativity. The power of a data set can be amplified by ingenuity through applications unimagined by the authors and distant from the original field."

In the United Kingdom, the Office of the Prime Minister in June 2009 announced that Tim Berners-Lee, founder of the World Wide Web, will "help drive opening of access to Government data on the web." Berners-Lee has been a leader of the open data movement, which aims to link government data with people's data in a web of linked open data systems built on W3C semantic web standards. Berners-Lee believes that this movement will lead to a quantum leap in the effectiveness, richness, and utility of the Internet. Many governments and government departments are now paying attention and opening their datasets accordingly. For example, it is currently possible to go to a website and see crime statistics for any borough, city, or area of the United Kingdom via an open dataset made available to the public by the police. This enables people to assess the crime risks involved in particular areas while enabling local governments to challenge the sometimes-incorrect assumptions about crime in areas as well as enabling communities to hold the police accountable for reducing crime. Similarly, it was the opening of the international space agencies' and militaries' GPS satellite systems that led to the development of many of the GPS navigational and location services common to us today.

Needless to say there will also be an increased need and pressure on enterprises to be transparent with their data in similar ways. Consumers will demand this, and companies will have to comply accordingly. Additionally, however, as with governments, the more progressive organizations will begin to see the benefits that can be achieved by being more transparent with their data, leading to new or improved commercial opportunities and hence competitive advantages. There is an irony in that pre-twenty-first-century business models encouraged companies to be more closed and restrictive with their information to retain competitive advantage, whereas twenty-first-century models will prove that those that are the most open and transparent with their data will receive the greatest returns.

It will also be important for people to be transparent with their data. The key advantages are going to come when we can combine disparate data systems. So linking government data with enterprise data and consumer data will yield the greatest insights. Many people will remain reluctant to share their personal data, but increasingly more and more people will be comfortable with doing so, owing to the benefits they will receive and the secure personal data management systems that will invariably emerge with Web 3.0. I believe the key to increased consumer transparency will be to put the control of people's data in their own hands, giving them control over who and what has access to it. Once people feel empowered as such, they will be more inclined to share their data with trusted third parties. This trend of openness, borderlessness, and interconnectedness will drive a cultural shift in the commercial and political landscape toward openness, resulting in more open corporate and social cultures. This is already the case in the political space, in that we generally associate openness with more advanced and progressive societies and being closed with repression and less progressive social models. These factors will continue to drive an increased need for organizations and governments to be more open with their customers and citizens.

The need for information to be atomized to its most granular form of data and for that data to be freely associated with other relevant and related data as per the semantic web model will also contribute to this increased need for transparency. The semantic web cannot truly come into being without high levels of transparency and freedom around data. This will certainly be a highly controversial subject for the next few years, owing to the exposed manner in which it will leave organizations and government institutions. It will also come under great pressure from consumer privacy groups that will oppose the absolute transparency of consumers' activities online, such as tracking and monitoring for behavioral targeting. Nonetheless, people will gradually become more and more comfortable with living in a more transparent and open manner online, and the trend toward increased openness and transparency will grow. This will be driven by both the cultural and technical needs aforementioned. We can already see this happening with Generation Y consumers and native netizens, who are more comfortable with sharing vast amounts of personal information about themselves online with their networks and with organizations. Again, I do believe this will remain a sensitive area for many more years and that many applications and services will emerge, enabling consumers some degree of protection and privacy. But overall I believe the web will drive us all toward much more open and transparent commercial, cultural, and social-political models than we have today and that this trend will irrevocably continue to grow as part of the Digitterran Tsunami.

1.18   Privacy

No review of the trends that will drive the Digitterran Tsunami would be complete without considering the rising concern of many people, organizations, and governments on the subject of privacy. There is already a high degree of concern from consumer and civil rights groups on the volume of data available on people to commercial and governmental bodies. This concern includes fears of being constantly monitored and being under surveillance to concerns about privacy and information rights. This anxiety is going to increase and become more potent in the Digitterran era, particularly in the early part of it.

There has been much discussion in the media and courts lately on this subject. A recent reaction to a bid by behavioral targeting advertising company Phorm in the United Kingdom is a prime example of this. Phorm was working with three of the United Kingdom's largest Internet service providers (ISPs)—BT, Virgin Media, and TalkTalk—to bring what Google would have called "Interest-based advertising" to the United Kingdom. The ISPs had planned to provide consumers' browsing-history data to Phorm. Phorm was to use this browsing history to deliver targeted advertising and content to consumers via its Webwise Discover application. Webwise allows content linked to what a consumer is or has been browsing to be displayed in a widget within the user's web browser, resulting in browsing sessions that are contextually rich and enabling users to find information more seamlessly.

However, the catch was that the ISPs were planning on providing this information to Phorm without the users' consent—and furthermore, they were not providing users with a means of opting out of the service. Worse yet, it emerged that BT and Phorm had carried out secret trials in 2006 and 2007 without users' knowledge or consent. Consequently, a huge backlash ensued, with consumer groups, including the Foundation for Information Policy Research (FIPR), a leading advisory group on Internet information use, declaring that Phorm's service was illegal. The European Union also moved to sue the UK government for its alleged failure to properly implement European privacy laws in the trials as specified within the union's ePrivacy Directive.

Tim Berners-Lee weighed in to condemn the notion of ISPs being allowed to intercept and profile their customers' Internet usage in a showdown with Kent Ertugrul, Phorm's CEO, in Britain's Houses of Parliament. Berners-Lee said, "It is very important that when we click we click without a thought that a third party knows what we're clicking on." BT, Virgin Media, and TalkTalk all eventually withdrew support for Phorm's Webwise Discover service, though all maintain that they are keen to continue to explore opportunities in the interest-based advertising space. Phorm also continued to run trials of its service with KT, South Korea's largest ISP, and with ISPs in fourteen other countries around the world.

In 2007 Facebook's CEO, Mark Zuckerberg, had to make a public apology on his blog for the disastrous launch of Facebook's Beacon advertising program. Beacon tracked the purchases of users on third-party sites and then pushed information of those purchases to the person's friends' pages on Facebook. The program drew the attention of Moveon.org, which gathered some seventy thousand signatures of displeased Facebook users claiming the service did not have an adequate opt-out function. Facebook quickly disabled the service and was forced to relaunch it later on an opt-in basis after backtracking to repair considerable damage the debacle caused its reputation. It was apparent that Facebook had not expected such a huge outcry from its customers over Beacon. It too had not understood how sensitive, suspicious, and passionate people are on the subject of privacy.

These examples highlight how volatile, political, and polarized the debate around privacy remains. This debate will invariably heat up as the potential to monitor people's activities and the benefits of being able to target content at ever more granular consumer profiles increase. As I mentioned previously in the discussion about the transparency principle, I believe the solution to this problem will be placing control of consumers' data in the hands of consumers and giving them full control over who has access to it and who does not, as well as control over what third parties can and cannot do with this data. This will force organizations to deal with consumers on consumers' terms. If data is a new form of currency, then it seems only fair that consumers should have control of how their currency is used and spent. Therefore, it is clear that as technology enables greater tracking, monitoring, and surveillance of people's activities, their concerns around privacy will rise and they will increasingly seek ways to shield themselves from unwanted observations. The importance of earning people's trust so that they are willing to share their data will be increasingly paramount.

1.19   Duality

Many of the principles we have explored thus far may appear to be in conflict with other Digitterran principles. At first glance, they may be seen as being somewhat polarized. The next Digitterran principle we will thus explore is that of duality.

One might take the principle of me-centricity and its idea that we are all going to be much more introspective and focused on our self-centric universes, compared it with the principles of planetarianism and social activism, which imply that we will have a more socially holistic view of the world with a more macro and philanthropic perspective on society, and see them as being contrary. One might also look at the principle of multipolarity and the diversity that it implies will be celebrated in the Digitterran era and compare it with the principle of convergence and its homogeneity of culture, data, and media, for example, and see them as polar opposites. We might look at the principle of transparency, which dictates that we will be living more open lives and will be happy to share data with our social networks, companies, customers, and citizens and compare it with the principle of privacy, which demonstrates how people will become ever more concerned with their personal information, habits, and actions being open and exposed to companies, governments, and unsolicited third parties, and rightly see them as juxtaposed.

This ambiguity or duality is in itself a principle that is going to be an important trend in the Digitterran era. There will be a perpetual duality apparent in most things. An understanding that people are complex, multidimensional beings that oscillate between somewhat polarized opposites, depending on their desires, needs, and situations, is going to emerge. These poles will effectively become more dynamic and relative, and we will move between them depending on the needs of the specific situation or the nature of the task in hand. So at some times there will be a need for us to be more multipolar and more diverse in our outlook, while at other times there will be a need for us to be more convergent and homogeneous in our perspective. Sometimes we will need to be more self-centric, and sometimes we will need to have a more planetary or borderless perspective. Like the theory of relativity, in a sense, sometimes we will behave like waves and sometimes we will behave like particles, and our behavior in itself may oscillate between opposite principles relative to the context of the moment. It will be important for organizations and systems to understand this and to embrace this duality in people in order to make sense of consumers and to be able to connect with them appropriately and effectively.

People will become much more comfortable with integrating opposed notions in ways that are rational and that make sense to them. People will find both macro and micro perspectives on things. We will have global perspectives on some issues and local perspectives on others. In some situations we will be very open and transparent with our information, but at other times we will be ruthlessly precious about our privacy. We will be able to move easily between these opposed positions as needed. The challenge will be for organizations to understand when and how we fluctuate between these poles and the catalysts that lead us to different states. A simple example of this might be an understanding that certain people are more receptive to advertising messages at a certain times of the day than others are. This "ideal advertising time" though might change across cultures, across age groups, across professions, etc. So a person who might be receptive to an advertising message in the evening may absolutely resent it in the morning. Someone who might be keen to support a social cause when referred to it by a friend on Facebook may find it invasive when approached via an e-mail while at work, and for other people vice versa. Hence the need to develop a rich understanding of people's complexities and diversity will be essential toward understanding how to effectively navigate around people's dualities.

Organizations too will become much more comfortable with duality and this idea of polarized opposites, with aligning organizational goals, for example, versus industry and social goals. Organizations will also increasingly define themselves in the gray area between poles, rather than from the absolute black or white positions at the poles. This will be a more challenging task for companies than people though, as they will be held to much greater accountability and scrutiny than consumers on their fluctuations between the poles. They will therefore need to have very clear understandings of where they stand on issues and why they take the positions that they do.

Taking the lead will be the concept that we live in a world of complex dualities, and that, while we might at times gravitate toward the absolutes, it's actually the middle ground between the poles that binds us together in a balanced sense of equilibrium. So equilibrium between these opposite poles will become a more prevalent principle around the world in the Digitterran era. This equilibrium will be represented by our comfort with duality. We will see this happen socially, commercially, philosophically, and politically.

1.20   Zeroing

Of all the Digitterran principles, zeroing is perhaps the most elusive and difficult to explain. Zeroing is the idea that in the Digitterran era, the concept of trending toward zero will take a central role in the models used to structure our societies and social-cultural relationships. As I have said previously, I believe a fundamental principle of the Digitterran era is that all things that can easily be provided and reproduced virtually will trend toward zero cost and things that are harder to duplicate electronically will command a premium. So music recordings, for example, will become freely available, but concerts and performances will command a premium. Films will become freely available, but theatrical and cinematic experiences will command a premium.

Zero is an interesting phenomenon, for it is both mathematical and philosophical. While it describes nothingness mathematically, philosophically it represents a nothingness that is close in proximity to infinity. Philosophically, zero and infinity can be seen as two sides of the same coin—polarized perspectives on the same phenomenon.

Zeroing will be at the forefront of the way in which we understand ourselves and the relationships we have with each other in the Digitterran era. For example, with zeroing we can see that the "digital" distance between anyone on the planet and us, i.e., that which prevents us from connecting and engaging with others, trends toward zero. What creates distances between us are the ideas we harbor, the cultures in which we immerse ourselves, and languages we have command of. The distancing impact of these phenomena will, however, as a result of technology trend toward zero too.

In the social-commercial world, the impact of zeroing will be more mathematical. For example, costs for goods and services in the Digitterran era will trend toward zero. We will see more and more high-value services being delivered to the market for free. This will initially be driven by the *freemiumization* model but will eventually extend far beyond that. Education and health information will be some of the services at the forefront of this movement. We will see education services and products delivered to children and people of the world with increasingly zero or low costs. Organizations such as the Khan Academy lead the way in proving this model currently. They will go from strength to strength and start a groundswell of similar movements in other sectors. The continued consumerization of personal DNA sequencing has already brought the price of decoding one's personal DNA down to a couple of hundred dollars from several thousand dollars, and these services will continue to trend toward zero costs to consumers. Companies will continue to find innovative ways to add value to such services in ways that enable them to generate revenues, but the trend will continue toward zero costs for high-quality products and services, which will drive an increase in the depth and breadth of services that are delivered to people for free in order for companies to remain relevant and competitive. Inherent within this principle is the fact that the costs to provide high-quality goods and services will also trend toward zero. Product and material innovations such as 3D printing and nanotechnology, along with an increasingly roboticized workforce, will accelerate this trend.

On the philosophical side, zeroing will unify leading-edge scientific thinking, such as quantum mechanics and general relativity, with the forefront in philosophical constructs in terms of definitions of self as outlined by the likes of Ray Kurzweil, Alvin Toffler, and Kevin Kelly and funnel them through the filter of a me-centric reality to provide people with a powerful model of infinite potential and capability.

Zeroing paradoxically will lead to a new culture and mind-set of abundance in resources, potential, and possibility. People will start to see themselves as zero points with infinite potential for connection to other zero points, as entities with infinite potential for influence and creativity. Zeroing is perhaps the most profound and fundamental Digitterran principle and the one most likely to produce the most significant changes in the fabric, structure, and dynamic of our world as a whole. Though this way of thinking and the science and philosophy that support it are still something of a weak signal in scientific and technology communities currently, it will gain pace and acceptance rapidly owing to the huge potential it will unleash in solving the problems of our world and in providing people with a framework to understand and exploit phenomena that has eluded us as a species to date. The Internet and its Digitterran Tsunami will rapidly accelerate the spread of this principle.

1.21 Imagination

We are quickly approaching a stage now in the evolution of our systems, society, and technologies where technologies are able to facilitate things that we never imagined possible before. Technology is also enabling things to happen much more rapidly than we previously envisioned. A fast-approaching scenario is one where the limiting factor in what we can achieve and do with our technologies is the imagination that we bring to our innovations. This is going to be an incredibly important component in the development of the digital system and is the basis of our last Digitterran principle, imagination.

The imagination, desire, and vision that we collectively as a species bring to the system will shape and determine what the system is able to do and drive the possibilities that emerge from it. As we have already touched on, the Internet has already enabled new possibilities in ways of working, collaboration, resource management, efficiency, creativity, and innovation than we have ever seen before. As a result of this, we are now required to think in new ways. We are going to have to address things from new perspectives. We are going to have to change a lot of our current mental paradigms in order to continue to be productive, to continue to innovate and excel in this environment, and to bring the best that is possible to the world from our system.

The web has effectively become Jung's collective consciousness, (Gestalt), our ability to collectively think. The imagination and visions that we feed this collective mind will in many ways determine its ability to be generative and abundant.

We will very shortly have the first crop of netizens, i.e., people who were born into a world with the Internet and therefore do not know a world without an Internet, moving into the workplace. They will eventually move into key positions, where they will start to shape the future and have an impact. They will eventually be creative and authoritative in terms of the way that the Internet machine is developed. They will have new paradigms and new perspectives. They will not have the legacy baggage that many of us of the older generation have in terms of the way things have been done and the way that things can be done. They will also not have our current mental perspective of what reality is and what is possible. One thing the Internet is showing us is that many more things are possible than we might have until recently thought. The web in many ways has proved that, that which we would have thought was impossible until recently has suddenly become possible.

Kevin Kelly spoke about this in his lecture on the first and next five thousand days of the web. He proposed that if anyone in the 1980s had suggested a system like the Internet, with all its current applications and services, would be developed and given to the world, effectively for free, the person would have been looked at as a lunatic or, at best, an idealistic dreamer. There was no technological, commercial, or social model that could support such a proposal. Yet here today we have a world with exactly that, while two or three decades ago we couldn't envision anything that could enable the Internet to become the phenomenon that it has become in such a short time. It simply seemed impossible. This is even evidenced by the scarcity of science fiction literature predicting our current Internet model. Hence, imagination and dreaming the art of the possible will be key to the next wave of Internet evolution.

Also being that the capabilities of the World Wide Web machine have dramatically improved from when it came into being fifteen years ago, the need for imagination becomes more poignant and urgent, because the ability to deliver on our ideas and dreams is even more incredible and far-reaching than previous iterations of the system had suggested. The Internet machine is at a critical point in its evolution. Its progress through today has been driven by visionary technologists. It is imperative now that artists, philosophers, and humanists join the effort to shape the mind of the machine so that it is taught elegance, ethics, and compassion. Imagination and dreams will be critical in shaping what we expect of our machine, which in turn will govern what it delivers to us.

Part II

Chapter 2   The NEO-Citizen

2.1 The Five Dimensions of Neo-Citizenship Rights

Fundamentally the Digitterran Tsunami is going to usher in a new type of world. The world that we live in will change dramatically, and a new world will emerge with a new type of inhabitant. I call this reorganization the new earth order (NEO) and the new inhabitants driving this change the NEO-citizens.

Citizens are the fundamental units and building blocks of all societies. Without citizens there are no societies, and societies are the creations of their citizens. Both need each other to exist. NEO-citizens will be the new citizens who emerge in societies around the world as a result of all the changes being driven by the Digitterran Tsunami. NEO-citizens will exploit the Digitterran principles outlined previously to amplify the Digitterran Tsunami and accelerate the earth's changes. At its core, NEO-citizenship will have five dimensions of rights attributed to it to it.

Global Citizenship

The first of these dimensions will be global citizenship. All people by nature of birth on planet Earth will have global citizenship rights. NEO-citizens will be actively aware of this. As we have outlined in the previous chapter, global citizenship rights will be a base level of human rights to which anyone born on the planet will be entitled. NEO-citizens will champion this, and they will drive an adoption of global citizenship rights through some sort of international treaty, which they will demand that their governments ratify in the same manner as the Geneva Convention and the Universal Declaration of Human Rights.

National Citizenship

Of course, they will also have national citizenship rights. All people are born into our current world within a framework where we have nation entities and where every piece of land on this planet (except Antarctica) is part of a nation-state. Most people born within a nation on earth have the citizenship rights of that nation. Many people also have dual national citizenship rights, and many more will do so as people continue to be more widely traveled and culturally integrated. Consequently all inhabitants of the planet will have global and national or binational citizenship rights.

Regional Citizenship

Then there will also be regional citizenship rights. For example, someone born in the United States may have North American Free Trade Agreement (NAFTA) citizenship rights, as well as US citizenship rights, as well as global citizenship rights. Someone born in Spain would have Spanish citizenship rights, as well as European Union citizenship rights, as well as global citizenship rights. So, many of the world's citizens will fall into regions, regional blocks, and regional clusters that will offer them citizenship rights by nature of their national citizenship. This trend has been on the rise for the past six decades with a move toward centralization and regionalization in global geopolitics. Being that some people will have dual national citizenship rights, they will also have dual regional citizenship rights. For example, I am a dual citizen of Nigeria and the United Kingdom. As such, I am also a dual citizen of the European Union and the Economic Community of West African States. In addition, by default of my Nigerian citizenship, I am also a citizen of the African Union.

Resident Citizenship

Local residency rights are another obvious right that people will have. These may not be as poignant or as legally binding as citizenship rights, but people will definitely have residency benefits and rights that are highly relevant to them according to the sub-national states, cities or the counties in which they live or the boroughs in which they live within cities.

I think we are going to see a return of the citylike states of medieval Italy as national boundaries and national infrastructures become less relevant and as we move more toward regional and global infrastructures. City and sub-national state entities will become more important. This again is corroborated by the urbanization trend that we see happening in the world today. According to the United Nation's 2007 World Urbanization Prospect report from the year 2010, for the first time in human history more of the world's inhabitants will live in cities than in rural areas:

> "Between 2007 and 2050, the world population is expected to increase by 2.5 billion, passing from 6.7 billion to 9.2 billion (United Nations, 2008). At the same time, the population living in urban areas is projected to gain 3.1 billion, passing from 3.3 billion in 2007 to 6.4 billion 2050. Thus, the urban areas of the world are

expected to absorb all the population growth expected
over the next four decades while at the same time

> *drawing in some of the rural population. As a result,*
> *the world rural population is projected to start*
> *decreasing in about a decade and 0.6 billion fewer*
> *rural inhabitants are expected in 2050 than today.*
> *Furthermore, most of the population growth*
> *expected in urban areas will be concentrated in the*
> *cities and towns of the less developed regions. Asia, in*
> *particular, is projected to see its urban population*
> *increase by 1.8 billion, Africa by 0.9 billion, and Latin*
> *America and the Caribbean by 0.2 billion. Population*
> *growth is therefore becoming largely an urban*
> *phenomenon concentrated in the developing world"*[9]

So not only are we becoming more urban, we are also changing the balance between urban living and rural living in an unprecedented way—meaning that more and more people will live in cities, and cities will have a greater role to play in terms of people's immediate rights. I believe in many ways the national model will disintegrate in two directions—toward more city-state-like infrastructures and toward more macroregional geopolitical infrastructures. City residency rights will become important local residential rights in this context.

---

[9] United Nations Department of Economic and Social Affairs, Population Division. "World Urbanization Prospects: The 2007 Revision." February 2008.

Virtual Citizenship

The most interesting dimension to NEO-citizenship from a Digitterran perspective, however, will be the rise of virtual citizenship rights. Citizenship in the world currently is primarily achieved by birth in or naturalization to a particular territory of land to which the nation providing those national rights has sovereign rights. However, when we look at the phenomenon of global warming and climate change, we can see that many nations of the world that exist currently are going to disappear from the earth in the near future owing to rising sea levels. Countries such as Tuvalu, Kiribati, the Federated States of Micronesia, the Marshall Islands, and the Maldives are all scheduled to disappear and to simply not exist anymore in as few as fifty years.

An interesting question is what happens to the citizens of those countries when their countries disappear? From that point onward, these people will become citizens of what will effectively be a virtual nation, a nation that existed previously but that no longer physically exists—above sea level, at least. A nation's territorial integrity is considered a primary legal principle of the modern world, and there is currently no legal definition for a country completely without land. There is also no record in history of a country losing its national boundaries without a military intervention. Tuvalu is also particularly interesting as it generates significant revenue from selling the rights to its national .tv Internet domain. With revenues, citizens, and no provisions for its residents to be repatriated to third-party countries, it cannot simply disappear as a nation. International law will have to modify how we demarcate and identify the national borders for states like this accordingly, and it seems inevitable that such predicaments will have to be resolved with virtual states.

This issue will converge on the Internet, and we will see virtual nations emerge with real-world citizens with real-world citizenship rights who live within host regions or within other countries on the planet. They may, for example, resolve to have dual national citizenship rights, one set from the nation in which they are forced to live and one set from their disappeared and now virtual nation. The important thing to recognize here is that, for the first time in history, there will be non-geo-nation territories. That is to say, we will have nations that are based around territories other than land.

Early embryos of these can be seen in some of the virtual worlds such as Second Life. In these worlds people are members of virtual communities with laws, rights, real-world currency-exchange networks, and virtual businesses. This phenomenon is a precursor to actual virtual states, whereby people have currency, political rights, political clout, leaders, and elections and all sorts of processes through which they can drive changes from the virtual world into the physical world. The emergence of virtual states is going to be a key dynamic of the Digitterran era. In these states, real people will combine and leverage their physical world rights with their virtual rights to bring about material changes in the world around us.

These thus are the structural pillars of NEO-citizenship that will emerge: global, regional, and national citizenship rights, local residency rights and virtual citizenship rights.

2.2 NEO-Citizenship—Principles and Values

That said, NEO-citizens will not simply be defined by their multidimensional and complex citizenship rights. They will also be defined by their principles, values, and actions in shaping a new social order.

An example of this can be seen in the area of consumption. NEO-citizens will consume in ways that can drive social change. NEO-citizens will understand that there is power in their consumption habits and behaviors and will use that to effect change from organizations. It is what is known as "mindful consumption" and is essentially about using purchasing power to endorse or reject a corporation. Furthermore, when combined with network effects, this can represent a significant commercial lever with which to reward or chastise companies. This is also known as "cooperative consuming." There are several current examples of people grouping together to incentivize organizations to make social changes, change policies, or change their operations and products in line with the group's needs. Carrotmobs are a great example of this. They are networks of consumers who have turned the boycotting model on its head to reward companies making the most socially responsible decisions. Consumers band together and combine their spending power to make the most socially responsible businesses the most profitable ones.

This can be a powerful motivator to companies and is a great resource for social entrepreneurs. It is thus easy to see that mindful consuming is going to be an important and powerful element of the NEO-citizen's profile. The NEO-citizen will therefore be a mindful and often cooperative consumer.

Social philanthropy will be another dynamic that will be very important to NEO-citizens. They will work toward better social care and will be sensitive to the needs of the more disenfranchised and poor of society. Many NEO-citizens will emerge as powerful philanthropists and social entrepreneurs.

Ecological guardianship will be another passion of NEO-citizens. They will be highly ecologically aware and informed. They will seek ecological balance and promote sourcing renewable technologies and renewable energies. They will use their citizenship powers to bring about ecological balance and changes. They will be self-proclaimed guardians of the planet's ecosystem.

They will also be world peace champions. NEO-citizens will very much understand that they are people of the world, and they will strive to achieve a balance of peace and an end to violent conflict. They will intercede and interject through their various political and social mechanisms to try to bring more peace into the world.

I also believe that NEO-citizens will generally advocate a higher degree of global tolerance. An appreciation of the dynamic of duality and an understanding of the polarized nature of life will lead NEO-citizens to a greater sense of awareness, tolerance, and acceptance of fellow mankind and of mankind's differences. NEO-citizens will be very diverse, and diversity will be at the core of the NEO-citizenship model. Multipolarity, interconnectedness, and codependence will also be central to the NEO-citizenship framework. As such, NEO-citizens will be tolerant, understanding, and respectful of different cultures and different worldviews while remaining uncompromising in their drive toward the establishment of a new order that seeks greater balance among cultures, peoples, and the ecosystem of the planet as a whole. NEO-citizens will be uberplanetarians.

World nutrition, the end of hunger, and global feeding championship will be another endeavor that NEO-citizens will adopt. Global human rights will be seen as basic liberties that NEO-citizens will passionately and actively pursue for all.

They will also be very driven and active about global education and the right of all people to education. They will be able to consumerize education and deliver it to all people around the world at low or no cost through virtual means. NEO-citizens will be very passionate in ensuring that all people of the planet have access to education, as education will lead to the empowerment of people and to growth in the numbers of NEO-citizens, which will in turn enable all to effect greater and more accelerated changes.

Health care will be another area in which we will see tremendous progress made by NEO-citizens. With advances in technologies, monitoring systems, self-diagnosing, and automedicating systems, we will see much more traction in the proliferation of reliable health care around the world to its masses of people.

NEO-citizenship will be about ensuring that all people's human rights and global citizenship rights are respected. These will include the right to food, water, and health care, as well as the right to education, to being able to speak one's mind freely without persecution by authorities, to shelter, and the right to peace.

I believe NEO-citizens will call for a Universal Bill of Digital Rights anchored to the Universal Declaration of Human Rights and will propose that the Internet enables many human rights to be delivered in more tangible ways than in the world before the Internet. They will defend the preservation of these rights for all.

Finland recently achieved a world first by declaring that all its citizens have a legal right to 1 megabit of broadband Internet access as of July 2010. (By 2015 the right will be extended to 100Mb.) NEO-citizens will seek to extend this right to global citizens as part of the Universal Bill of Digital Rights. After all, it is the connectedness of the world's citizens that empowers each citizen in the Digitterran era. As such, getting all people of the world online will be an important goal for NEO-citizens and organizations of the Digitterran era.

NEO-citizens will be active in the areas mentioned above for a variety of reasons. Firstly, they will become more socially active, as we have discussed, because it will be much easier for them to do this than it has been in the past. We can see from the political campaigns of Howard Dean and Barack Obama that if people are given the tools that make it easy for them and they are inspired with the right kind of call to action, they will enthusiastically rally around a cause and work tirelessly to achieve it. Digital technologies will make it increasingly easy for people to be social activists. Additionally, a raft of social entrepreneurial business models will emerge that incentivize and reward people for their activism.

People will also be socially active because they will be encouraged to do so by their network of friends and influencers. Many of the people in their networks will be involved in many of the causes we have just outlined and similar socially progressive causes. As such, people will be increasingly encouraged and supported in their social responsibility activities by their networks of peers. We see simple examples of this today in people running marathons or going on long walks for charities and raising sponsorship from their families and friends. It will become increasingly popular for people to do these sorts of activities and lobby support from their social networks. Additionally, it will be increasingly "cool" for people to be social activists of some sort and to contribute to the resolving of major social and world issues such as hunger, clean water, and education for all. This too will be a powerful motivator for people to get involved.

Finally people will also want to get involved with causes because it will give them a great sense of satisfaction and will make them feel good. They will enjoy being able to help people around the world or in their communities and will enjoy coming to the help of others. Like all other movements online, once a tipping point is reached, they swell up from the grassroots and gain an ever-increasing momentum and dynamic from the world's citizens. That is to say once a critical mass of people starts to think and operate like this, there will be an exponential expansion and huge groundswell, and the movement will rapidly grow in size and momentum. Very much like a tsunami!

So we can see a dual phenomenon unfolding. The increase in NEO-citizens and the rise of the Digitterran Tsunami will both converge to change the world. NEO-citizens will feed the Internet machine that's driving this tsunami with the information, ethical code, and moral compass with which the tsunami will grow. The Digitterran Tsunami, by the same token, this wave of innovation and change, will provide NEO-citizens with the infrastructure, resources, and momentum to manifest the changes they envision in the world. Both will form a digital and social ecosystem of codependence and change.

The Decline of the Nation-State

Nation-states will become less and less relevant to NEO-citizens. Many authors have written over the past two decades on the diminishing importance, power, and relevance of the nation-state. Most notable of these authors would be Kenichi Ohmae, who among other things is credited with coining the term *globalization*. Ohmae has led the thinking on the rise of the regional hub as opposed to the nation-state. Interestingly, the nation-state is a relatively modern phenomenon. At the turn of the twentieth century, there was a sum total of fourteen nation-states in the world. With the expansion of the colonial era, this number grew exponentially as large continents and regions of the planet were carved into national territories that enabled equilibrium of power to be maintained among the handful of colonial states that led the colonization of the new worlds. With the independence movement of the '60s, most of these nation-states established autonomous political entities with their own governments and citizenship. This social-political order has remained in place since then till now. The relevance of these national infrastructures is becoming increasingly questionable in a digitally connected and consumer-centric world. Owing to advancements in transportation and communication technologies, people are able to move around regions and continents more easily in many ways than they had been able to do previously. The Internet has given billions of people the means of remaining in contact and regularly communicating with friends, family, and associates across the world. This has meant that people have become more informed on opportunities, differences, and indeed similarities between where they are and other places where they might like to be. Much of the world is accessible to those who have the determination and conviction to seek a better and perhaps different life in another part of it.

Culture has also become extremely portable in the modern world, to the extent that people tend to share more in common across psychographics than across demographics. Teenagers in Moscow and Shanghai are more likely to have similar interests and pursuits with teenagers in Sao Paulo or Johannesburg than, say, young professionals in Saint Petersburg or Beijing. This in itself is nothing new or unique from other eras. What does, however, make the current era unique is that it is now more likely for teenagers across the world to be sharing and consuming the same media. Also, it is astonishingly easy for such teenagers to create tribes, groups, clans, or networks of like-minded teenagers who are not limited by geographic, political, or social barriers as they were in the last century. This is going to increasingly become the case. In the next wave of the Internet, even cultural walls such as language will become less effective on dividing like-minded people. We are already seeing a much greater exchange of ideas, media, and experiences across national borders by everyday people. In the previous century, most of these transnational cultural exchanges were facilitated by the international media networks, film distribution companies, elite education institutions, and the small, fragmented person-to-person communications of telephone calls and letters. The Internet, however, has allowed people in disparate locations to maintain open networks through which they can exchange ideas, media, information, and experiences at the speed of light. With these come new cultural alliances as people within these networks start to feel greater cultural affinity with those in their virtual networks than they do with those in their physical environments. This is particularly the case when these virtual networks are organized around principles and interests about which the members are particularly passionate and driven.

Needless to say, national identity has a great depth of meaning to many people and will not simply disappear with the emergence of Internet technologies. In fact, the Internet is more of a contributor to the declining nationalist movement than a driver of it. We can see several social economic factors driving to the disintegration of nationalism and the rise of regionalism. Examples would include free trade agreements between regional states, regional currencies, regional media platforms, regional citizenship, regional NGOs, etc. It is against this backdrop that we see the power of virtual networks rising, which will further contribute to the eroding importance of the nation-state to its citizenship. This is a principle that we will revisit from several vantage points in this series of books as we proceed.

The Rise of the Virtual State

Central to the Digitterran Tsunami and the rise of the NEO-citizen will be the concept of the virtual state. This phenomenon perhaps more than any other will accelerate our evolution from land- and bloodline-based social organizations to idea and principle-based ones. Though this may sound farfetched, it is both inevitable and imminent. We have already explored the evolution of *phyles* or neo-tribes with the principle of NEO-tribalism. The virtual state will bring the NEO-tribal principle to its apex and will accord these social units material political power. To understand the inevitability of this phenomenon, we can again look at the disappearance of numerous island states owing to global warming and rising sea levels.

According to Lillian Yamamoto and Miguel Esteban of the United Nations University, *It is unclear what the status of an Island state would be if its entire territory were to be submerged. This is an essential problem as it would bring into question the island's ability to exploit its Exclusive Economic Zone (EEZ) which is the part of the sea around the island to which the state has special rights regarding the use and exploitation of marine resources as outlined in United Nations* Convention on the Law of the Sea *(UNCLOS). It would also call into question the ability and right of the nation to preserve the cultural identity of its citizens. The right of the citizens to dispose of their wealth and resources would be violated a right provided by Art. 1(2) of the* International Covenant on Civil and Political Rights*: "In no case may a people be deprived of its own means of subsistence."* They go on to say, *The loss of all the territory of a State would result in the deprivation of a means of subsistence for the population. In addition, if their governments do not make arrangements to keep their institutions working, the population could become stateless. Indeed, it could be argued that atoll island States* [such as Tuvalu, which is soon to disappear under water] *and cultures can never be satisfactorily compensated for the loss of their physical bases.*[10]

These scenarios are making the case for the recognition of virtual states that do not necessarily have physical borders.

Furthermore, I believe that the principle of popular sovereignty, *the idea that the legitimacy of a state is created and maintained by the will of its people who are the sources of all political power*[11] and which is the foundation of all modern nations, empowers people to create such virtual states as internationally recognized political entities to protect their needs and interests as required.

Let's look at it from a human rights perspective. As I have stated previously, I believe that there is a clear and legitimate case to be made for establishing a Universal Bill of Digital Rights that protects human rights in the digital age. (A draft proposal for such a bill can be found as an appendix.) This theory is based on the following assumptions. The Universal Bill of Human Rights details de facto global citizenship rights. These rights should protect every child born into the world today, so they are in effect global

[10] Atoll islands and climate change: disappearing States? *Lillian Yamamoto and Miguel Esteban*
[11] Wikipedia

citizenship rights. A Universal Bill of Digital Rights will make many human rights more tangible and enforceable in the digital age.

Furthermore, the Universal Declaration of Human Rights and the proposed Universal Bill of Digital Rights outline the right of global citizens to establish entities for the purpose of monitoring, upholding, and maintaining these rights. The principle of popular sovereignty means that such entities would have the *sovereign* right to protect and maintain such rights of their citizens on a global basis if a global people provided them with the mandate to do so by their consent.

So in short, if the people decide to establish a sovereign virtual state to protect and maintain their digital rights, it is difficult to see how international law will prohibit such a state from being established and recognized, other than preventing it from coming into being on the basis that it has no physical land or borders. But again as we have seen, the need for nonphysical states is clear and immediate based on the disappearance of several island states due to global warming. Even if the international community were to deny sovereignty owing to the absence of physical borders, the logical alternative would be to establish a virtual state with a micronation for the physical core of the state with the aim of becoming a microstate with citizenship being granted to anyone who agreed to abide by the state's constitution and wished to become a citizen of the state via the Internet. Again, scale and size do not determine the viability of this in cyberspace. The quality of the idea is what counts.

Physical space and time mean little and are less of a barrier to success in cyberspace than they are in the physical world.

Though most of the few micronations in existence today are somewhat irreverent and none is recognized as a sovereign state by the international community, if such an entity were to amass a large enough following and were to establish a fundamental *raison d'etre,* such as protecting human rights, it would be hard to see how it would not eventually be accorded some degree of international recognition. Its citizens will demand it of their leaders and the international community as a whole. It is on the basis that I see the rise of virtual states as being not only inevitable but also imminent.

With the establishment of such entities, mankind would have taken a significant social evolutionary step forward. For the first time in our history as a species, we would be able to establish sovereign states that could protect and promote a culture and citizenship that was not based on land, bloodlines, heritage, or location but on ideas, principles, and goals alone. This will be a tremendous achievement and a critical milestone in the rise of NEO-citizens.

Part III

Chapter 3   The Historic Context

3.1   The Information Revolution

Much has been written from the earliest days of the Internet on its role in driving the information revolution. Contrary to some beliefs though, the information revolution did not begin with the arrival of the Internet or World Wide Web. One could argue that the information revolution truly began with spoken language and wall painting. It was with language and painting that our earliest ancestors were able to collate ideas and packets of raw data into information that could be passed from one human being to another.

The next major breakthrough in the information revolution came with writing. It was with writing that information and indeed knowledge could be gathered collated, packaged, and passed on from on person to many others, remotely. This has been a key building block of civilization, allowing man to share ideas, concepts, knowledge, and findings and, perhaps more important, to build on that pool of knowledge by allowing one person or group of people to explore the succinct and accurate ideas of others and to build upon them. This is what has enabled most of our advances as a species in the sciences and arts and is what has given us the building blocks on which to construct our ever-growing pool of concepts, theories, works of art, entertainment, innovation, invention, etc. That said, with the invention of writing, the spread of information did not have as dramatic an impact on the information revolution as speech had done, for writing and indeed reading were very specialized skills in their early days.

Speech, in contrast, quickly became ubiquitous and pervasive with all people across all cultures and thus represented a truly revolutionary leap in our journey along the information highway. However, speech was not a particularly reliable way of spreading information in a consistent manner. Writing, on the other hand, allowed information to be contained and in a sense kept in a solid state. It allowed information to remain stable and to be consumed by those who could decode it in a relatively consistent manner. Of course, true meaning or knowledge could be shrouded by hidden meanings and codes. But the raw information contained in documents and books was available to anyone who could decode the symbols used to represent the words regardless of where or whom that person was so long as the reader understood the language in which the text was written and the symbol system used to represent that language in writing. Hence the information being conveyed in the words in a text such as a constitution or a religious scroll could be understood by anyone who could read, even if the person was not necessarily informed enough to decode the deeper, sometimes hidden meanings behind the words. The reader could understand the surface-level information represented by the words.

The drawback, though, was that reading and writing were highly specialized skills practiced mostly by academics, the clergy, and the most privileged ranks of societies. Hence reading and writing were means of sharing information among small, controlling factions of society. Even with this, many early books and works of writing were written in coded language so that even if an unintended person who had the reading skills were to come across such writings, the reader would not be able to decode the hidden meaning or knowledge. This is similar to how one might come across a classic Newtonian equation such as Force = Mass x Acceleration and not be able to decipher any meaning from these words without having an understanding of Newtonian physics.

Reading and writing really became revolutionary on a mass global scale only with the invention of the printing press. With the printing press, written information became available to anyone who could learn how to read. This represented a huge expansion in mankind's ability to package, share, and consume information and really marked the beginning of the modern information revolution.

Though the word *paper* derives from the Greek term for ancient Egyptian writing material, papyrus, the immediate precursor to modern paper is believed to have originated in China around 105 CE. Paper and printing are considered two of the four great inventions of ancient China (gunpowder and the compass being the others). The Chinese invention of woodblock printing at some time around 868 CE is credited with producing the world's first printing system. Printing technology further advanced in China in the eleventh century with Bi Sheng's invention of the ceramic moveable-type press. However, owing to the huge volume of ancient Chinese characters (over one hundred thousand), moveable-type technology was somewhat impractical and inefficient for printing Chinese books. Consequently, most Chinese publishers continued to use woodblock printing presses to produce books, as it was less tedious and Chinese characters did not require strict alignment of characters, which moveable-type presses were best suited to achieving. There were thousands of such woodblock books produced in China with subjects from Confucian classics and articles of state, to books on medicine, science, and mathematics. As such, the world's first printing culture was born in China and quickly spread to neighboring countries, including Korea and Japan. That said, even the invention of the printing press in China in the ninth century did not immediately spur a truly quantum leap in the information revolution. This happened only when the technology was exploited in Europe in the fifteenth century.

In 1436 Johannes Gutenberg partnered with Andreas Dritzehn to develop a moveable-type printing press that was to revolutionize information sharing around the world. His invention exploited Chinese technologies with additional flat-pane pressing technologies that had gained in sophistication during several hundred years of development in Europe. The relative simplicity of the Latin alphabet and its need for precise alignment made moveable type an extremely effective and efficient means of printing European language texts. As a result, the invention of the Gutenberg press led to a quantum leap in the advancement of the information revolution across Europe. Gutenberg's press was comparable to the invention of the alphabet or writing in Europe. Within fifty or sixty years of its invention, the entire classic cannon had been printed and dispersed across Europe. Now that this information was so much more readily available, it could be discussed and debated by old and young readers alike. Also, as knowledge became popularized there was a sharp decline in the use of Latin to write, and books became written in local vernacular languages, enabling more people to read their contents. The printing press thus became a lead enabler in the democratization of knowledge and the driver of a social revolution among the masses.

Prior to the press the names of the authors of many books were simply lost. Books were not stable, and one book on Plato or medicine in London might be different from a supposed copy of the same book in Paris or Florence. The printing press bought new possibilities in consistency, and as such it became possible to reference books more easily. It also became more important to know who wrote books. Consequently, authors rose in prominence and profitability. With the commercial successes of print also came copyrighting and the intellectual property model we have today. This consistency was also critical in establishing the community of scientists who could now publish stable theses, which could be debated and developed by their peers without fear of being misrepresented or misquoted. Indices and indexing became possible too, with mass print runs enabling people to reference pages and sections within books, as for the first time one book, newspaper, or journal would be exactly the same as another copy of it. Hence the Gutenberg press was really the progenitor of mass communication media. It was the first means of distributing stable and consistent messages to massive numbers of people reliably.

Hot on the heels of printed material came radio communications. These included telegrams, radios, faxes, and telephones. These technologies were key in accelerating the speed at which information could be transferred from one part of the world to another. Radio broadcasts also became valuable ways of sharing information with the masses as they could deliver news, information, and entertainment in easy-to-consume and somewhat immediate formats to mass audiences. With radio, people simply had to listen to broadcasts as opposed to read them. This enabled people to consume content while they did other things such as cook, work, or drive. Telephones were also critical and noteworthy inventions in this class, as they were the first widely available technology to enable people to communicate directly with each other over distances since the letter, with the significant added advantages of being bidirectional, instantaneous, and in real time.

The next stage on the epic journey was film. Film enabled imagery and sound to be distributed to massive audiences across whole nations and internationally. Then came television, which enabled the same thing to be done directly to people in their homes, cementing itself at the heart of people's everyday lives. TV, radio, and print very quickly became the primary and ubiquitous means of disseminating and consuming information by most of mankind across the planet. A vibrant entertainment, news, and advertising industry built up around these mediums, owing to their ability to guarantee the attention of large audiences. Even today the vast majority of people consume large amounts of information through all three of these mediums on a regular if not daily basis. It was into this world that the Internet was born and into this world that the World Wide Web would lead to the next big jump in the information revolution of mankind.

The web enabled all previous information-disseminating mediums to coexist with many news ones in a single medium. Language, imagery, text, speech, music, and video could suddenly be disseminated and consumed over vast distances by anyone with Internet access and a basic computer. Though the system was originally quite slow and clunky, it quickly gained speed, meaning that vast amounts of data could be transported very easily across the globe quasi-simultaneously. This really took the information revolution to a new level of expansiveness and its logical conclusion. Suddenly any piece of information that anyone developed could be coded in a textual description, image, sound, video file, or some sort of data format that could be shared with other people who might be anywhere in the world with the simple use of an information-digitizing device such as a digital camera, a scanner, or microphone and a personal computer with an Internet connection.

Nowadays one does not even need the latter, as many mobile phones are capable of not only downloading information but also of uploading it in multiple formats to the Internet. As such there has been a true explosion of information and entertainment available to all people at their fingertips anywhere they are in the world at anytime of day, on demand. So expansive has been this explosion that at the turn of the twenty-first century, one of the most commercially successful businesses to emerge into this world has been Google, a company that provides people with a means of finding information they are seeking from the fifty billion pages of information currently available over the Internet. The Internet has become the ultimate information repository and one that continues to grow exponentially as it matures and increases its performance and penetration across our world and lives. No other medium has exposed so many people to so much information in all of mankind's history.

3.2   The Knowledge Revolution

The simple model for the transition of data to knowledge is this: Packets of data are gathered and clustered into packets of information. Packets of information are gathered and clustered into packets of knowledge. Packets of knowledge can be said to gather into clusters of expertise. As such it is my belief that the information revolution ends with the Internet. The information revolution is now giving way to the next wave in our journey, the knowledge revolution.

In the same way that the information revolution began with language, images, writing, and reading, so did the knowledge revolution. The difference was that while packets of data were collated into meaningful clusters, which could be consumed as information in the information revolution, packets of information are collated into meaningful clusters, which can be consumed as knowledge in the knowledge revolution. Since clusters of information are the building blocks of knowledge, it is clear that the big jumps in the information revolution also represent turning points in the knowledge revolution. As the information revolution has now peaked with the arrival of the Internet and its World Wide Web, the Internet is also facilitating the next big leap in our evolution as a social species, the knowledge revolution. Thus part of the next wave of the digital revolution will be the evolution of the Internet from a medium for aggregating and distributing vast amounts of disparate information into a medium for aggregating and sharing interrelated clusters of information—i.e., knowledge, accessible to all on demand. This will form the basis of a fundamental shift from a socioeconomic model that is based on adding value by producing things to one based on adding value by creating viable concepts and using knowledge. This is fundamentally different from the industrial model of the pre-twenty-first century and is a topic on which much has been written.

Marilyn Ferguson provides a description of the knowledge revolution in *The Aquarian Conspiracy (1980)*. She describes it as the ascendance of an irreversible shift in the global state of mind, a fundamentally new worldview that encompasses insights from ancient times through current breakthrough science. Charles Savage in his book *5th Generation Management (1990)* develops this idea further, suggesting that the shift is one of attitudes, values, and norms. He demonstrates that it will come only through a struggle of thought and proposes that many of the changes are counterintuitive from a traditional point of view and that they are difficult to conceptualize with industrial-era vocabulary. He also notes that a transition to a knowledge-centric culture will not be a simple or cumulative process, as new principles will need to be learned and some old principles will need to be unlearned. John Seely Brown in *The Knowledge Advantage (1999)* also advises that creating new frameworks for the evolving world will require challenging the assumptions that support our traditional intellectual constructs.

George Gilder in *Microcosm: The Quantum Revolution in Economics and Technology (1989)* provides a simple yet compelling description of the knowledge revolution. He says that the basic tenet of the knowledge revolution will be the "overthrow of matter." Wealth in the form of physical assets will diminish, while wealth in the form of knowledge assets will increase. The power of mind will supersede the brute force of things. Similarly, Jeremy Rifkin in *The Age of Access (2000)* states that whereas the industrial age emphasized the exchange of goods and services, the knowledge age will emphasize the exchange of concepts. David Brown in his book *Cybertrends (1997)* goes on to state that the knowledge revolution will not flow from the mobilization of new machines; rather it will require a fundamental revamp of the human context in which machines are used.

So we can see the knowledge revolution represents a significant departure from the current social-economic model of industrial production. A new model is emerging, with an economy based on knowledge and expertise transforming the commercial landscape we have inherited from the industrial era. This is not to say that there will no longer be any industries, as there inevitably will be. People will still need products, and industries will still have to produce them. The value proposition, however, in commercial enterprises will come in the knowledge space versus the production space. Kenichi Ohmae in *The Borderless World (1990)* illustrates that the average cost of manufacturing a product today is typically 25 percent of the end-user price. Production adds very little value in the eyes of consumers. He explains that it is just labor that rarely adds more value than it costs. He also notes with the advent of "steel collar workers" (robots), labor costs are becoming commoditized. Hence the value-adding area in the twenty-first century value chain is in the intellectual capital—the knowledge resources as opposed to the physical resources that go into producing things.

This puts a whole new emphasis on the importance of the Internet as a knowledge-aggregating and -sharing system. It puts the Internet at the heart of all twenty-first-century enterprise. Some might argue that we are already seeing models of such enterprises with companies such as Twitter and Facebook that have secured millions of dollars in start-up capital based on their ability to potentially aggregate information and knowledge for consumers. Google, one of the wealthiest companies on the planet, has a primary business proposition of being able to provide meaningful and relevant information to consumers. These are not companies of the industrial era. They are companies that place a paramount importance on being able to provide people with useful and relevant knowledge and interactions. They look and operate much more like pioneering companies of the digital knowledge era.

3.3   Web 1.0

The birth of the World Wide Web in 1994 was the beginning of a phenomenon that has since changed the commercial, social, cultural, and political fabric of our planet. The web's evolution to date can be categorized as two waves. The first of these was the birth of the World Wide Web from the Internet, which we will refer to as Web 1.0. The second was the evolution of the web after the 2001 stock market crash to its current state, Web 2.0. In this chapter we are going to explore the difference between Web 1.0 and Web 2.0. That said, there are many great books that have been written that describe Web 1.0 and Web 2.0 eloquently and accurately. I will not attempt to duplicate these but will simply give a high-level summary of the key drivers and facets of the Internet's two waves of innovation to date. A good place to start therefore would be a definition of what Web 1.0 was and how it differs from Web 2.0. The book itself is about Web 3.0, and its introduction concludes with a high-level description of what I see as the key differences between Web 1.0, 2.0, and 3.0.

Culture

The first perspective from which we will review Web 1.0 is its impact on culture. Culturally we can see that Web 1.0 was a new communication phenomenon. It was the birth of what has been labeled the information superhighway. With Web 1.0 we suddenly had a new means with which people could share information and connect with other people around the world quickly. So one of the first impacts of the Web was the internationalization of information. With the birth of the web, information could be published to a global audience and travel around the world quasi-instantly. At this stage the web was definitely seen as a new mass market and mass communication tool. It allowed companies, organizations, and governments to communicate with lots of people, both nationally and internationally, and to reach people whom they hitherto had been unable to engage directly. This connecting with consumers directly around the world through a new and exciting modern channel was an important principle of Web 1.0. Corporations, in many ways, were at the forefront of this, and the commercial world really led the way. Governments quickly followed suit though and endeavored to publish information about their activities and to use the web to communicate with their constituents and citizens. Several government information websites were launched, and the web was seen as a way of making government information readily available to the public.

Another aspect of Web 1.0 versus the world before the World Wide Web was this idea of rich information. With the web it became possible for companies and governments to give customers a lot of rich information and detail about their products and services in a way that they weren't really able to do before. Television advertising was always very limited, and unless people went and actually sought out specific information about a company via brochures or other forms of corporate literature, they could not really get access to detailed company information. There was also a time lag to people getting such information. They would either have to wait to receive it in the mail or go to a branch, store, commercial facility, or library to get the information they sought. Web 1.0 changed this and enabled companies and organizations to publish information that could be retrieved and read by customers with web access whenever they wanted quasi-instantly. For this reason Web 1.0 was very much about companies taking the traditional brochure and literature and publishing it on the web. In fact, the term often used to define Web 1.0 approaches to website design is "brochureware," where companies publish websites that are effectively brochures of their products and services. Initially, companies quite literally just took the files that they had for their brochures and published them online, using the same sort of graphics and the same design templates. Eventually people began to understand that the Internet was a different type of medium from printed literature. An understanding began forming that businesses had to repurpose their content or structure it slightly differently for the Internet, as people read content on the Internet differently from how they read printed material. Newspapers, for example, were quite progressive in this period. They restructured online articles by putting short introductory paragraphs to stories, understanding that people's attention span was different online and that the size of the real estate of the screen was different from what they were used to. Teaching clients how to repurpose content from their libraries in efficient ways ergonomic to online consumers was an important task for early Internet consultants.

From a consumer's point of view, the big, exciting thing about the rise of the World Wide Web was the idea of surfing. The Internet was promoted as a new realm—a huge cyberspace—that one could surf through, going from page to page or place to place and discovering exciting and useful information. Surfing was seen as going on an electronic journey. Surfing the web, you could learn different things about different places and different companies and experience the world in this new cyber way. "Virtual reality" was another term that was very popular at the time, and it suggested one could go and experience organizations and places in some sort of exciting, technologically enabled way.

The early days of the Internet were dominated by a combination of text and photographic imagery. That said, though it was all very static in the early days, one of the exciting things about Web 1.0 was that it brought the idea of multimedia to the fore, that people and organizations could express and communicate with each other in a much richer format than simple text and still imagery. Rich media became a poignant principle with Web 1.0, showing we could have text, images, animations, video, and sound. There were technical limitations, primarily around bandwidth and access costs, so audio and video were not as prevalent as text and images in the early days. It also became important to know how to reduce image file sizes so that they could download quickly. Bandwidth was one of the big chokers with Web 1.0.

Commerce

Commercially, the early Internet was delivered via a subscription model that used per-minute or per-byte billing. People paid either for the amount of data that they downloaded or for the amount of time that they spent online. Most Internet service providers (ISPs) had commercial models that were based around this notion, and people became cautious of how much time they spent online, owing to the costs.

From a marketing perspective, companies saw an opportunity to expand their brand message through Web 1.0. It continued previous twentieth-century branding and marketing philosophies of brands defining themselves by "packaging" abstract conceptual pillars that reflected the essence of the brand into messages, and then pushing those message out to a mass market via mass media to as many people within a targeted demographic profile as possible. With Web 1.0, companies continued to have a controlled brand messaging approach, similarly to how they had done before. It required them to repurpose that message slightly for a new medium but did not initially require them to think about marketing in a different way. All the same, many companies struggled to understand the best way to tweak the presentation of their message for this new channel, and an industry of agencies that could help them understand this and develop "on-brand" websites to express their brands was born. These sites maintained the traditional one-way approach; brands broadcast messages to consumers, and consumers consumed the messaging given to them appropriately. This messaging consumption influenced people's purchasing behavior as before.

The idea that the owner of the brand reserved all rights was still maintained, in the context of how brands structured their intellectual property spilling over from the previous twentieth-century model and approach. In a marketing culture context, early Web 1.0 was really just an extension of marketing business as usual; there was just a new channel added to the mix. What did start to change though was the way of selling things. E-commerce was born as security and payment systems became evolved enough for people to feel safe and comfortable buying and selling things online. Sales started to change dramatically, and a new science of online advertising and marketing emerged as a way of selling things primarily to people over the Internet.

With this commercial impetus, the Internet became a huge phenomenon and a raft of commercial activity sprung up around the idea of being an Internet-friendly company. There became a stampede to register domain names and add .com to brand names. For example, Reuters' share price jumped when it announced it was renaming itself Retuers.com, and Time Warner—one of the oldest and largest media companies in the world—merged with a fledgling AOL. The valuation of Internet companies accelerated at an incredible pace. A lot of companies presented themselves as Internet businesses and were able to secure high multiples of funding, based on ideas that had no validation or verification at that point. Companies were being valued for millions of dollars without business models, product strategies, or any of the essentials of business as known. Many became so highly valued by the mere fact that they had become Internet "compatible," or Internet businesses, that there was a huge overvaluation in the marketplace. Consequently, the market corrected and readjusted itself in what became known as the dot-bomb market collapse of 2000, and US$8 trillion of wealth evaporated into virtual smoke.

Needless to say, there were also many success stories. The Amazons, eBays, Yahoos!, and Googles of the world, nascent Web 2.0 companies born in the Web 1.0 era, emerged, epitomizing the new way of doing business and selling things. Amazon became a phenomenal retailer of books, whereby people could effectively order things from their living room. People were suddenly able to buy products and services online in their own time when they wanted. It spread at a phenomenal rate, and e-commerce became a burgeoning industry. What was also interesting about the e-commerce phenomenon was that all the projections of the major Internet companies of 1999–2001, in terms of how e-commerce would expand, were met—even with the collapse of the market. It is important to note there was a lot of accuracy in the projections and expectations for the growth of e-commerce. Where the difference lay was in the overvaluation of companies based on uniformed speculation by investors desperate to get in on the dot.com wave.

It was in fact following the crash of the market in 2001 that Tim O'Reilly coined the term Web 2.0. It was a way of stating that Internet companies had actually done their due diligence in reporting on e-commerce figures and that the Internet would rise from the ashes of the dot.bomb implosion and come to play an important role as a business platform.

Web 1.0 culture was a technology-centric phenomenon led by technocrats. People who understood technology and computers were really at the forefront with the birth of Web 1.0. Any website that was developed had to have a webmaster, someone who had effectively mastered the Internet and was the conduit or gatekeeper for content going onto the website.

Culturally, Web 1.0 also enabled rapid communication. E-mail was born, and with it came the ability to send messages around the world at the speed of light. While the fax machine had allowed us to send rapid messages before, it was never with the convenience of just being able to type something up on your computer and dispersing it anywhere in the world at the click of a key. E-mail also allowed people to send images and rich multimedia files in high fidelity. Shortly after e-mail came instant messaging, which enabled two or more people to hold an instant conversation over the net via a common messaging client. Unlike sending an e-mail, which was generally perceived as a letter that required action or a response, instant messaging was more of a casual or less structured real-time conversation held online. In parallel with this emerged SMS, or text messaging, as it is known. SMS meant that people could send from the keyboard of their cell phones short messages that appeared almost immediately on the cell phones of others. Even though it was initially used much more locally and nationally, people soon realized that the technology too was a way to keep in touch internationally.

All these technologies swept in a new openness of communication. Suddenly people around the world were able to talk to each other in very easy and accessible ways. Text, instant messaging, and e-mail gave people instantaneous written conversation exchange mechanisms and created a culture of immediacy in terms of communication still prevalent today. They also brought a new internationalization of communication to the world. Prior to the web, international communications among everyday people primarily happened via the mail system or with telephone calls. The Internet brought a variety of new ways for people to converse directly with each other in real and quasi-real time all over the world.

This international element was an echo of the interactive phenomena that Web 1.0 introduced to the marketplace. Web 1.0 introduced the idea that one could have content with which one could interact, and one could go from one piece of content to another and explore storylines or message lines and surf around from one island of information to another land of information—including information from foreign lands. As such, a cultural phenomenon began to emerge with Web 1.0—the idea that we could be much more internationalized, communicating and connecting with people around the world very rapidly, via the Internet. We started to grasp a rich interactive cyberspace and virtual reality with which we could tap into and connect with the rest of the online world. We knew that this new medium would bring new models of socializing and working that were only beginning to make sense to most of us.

Information

At the information level, Web 1.0 really represented the birth of the information superhighway, the peak of the information revolution, and the beginning of the knowledge revolution. With Web 1.0, vast amounts of information suddenly became available to anyone with a computer and a modem. This availability and accessibility of content was one of the key informational principles of Web 1.0. Web 1.0 could also be described as the period when most information became electronically published. E-publishing was a principle of Web 1.0, as was information being available on demand. The cost of publishing content online was minuscule in comparison with printing information in the pre-

Internet era. As such, companies and organizations became much more liberal about publishing information.

Soon people started to realize the exposure entailed by so much information being available, and some people became more guarded and closed about what was published. Obviously, there were many organizations that were always extremely cautious and conservative in deciding which information could be published, but overall, a lot of information became available to the masses via Web 1.0. The sudden availability of large amounts of information to the world really characterizes the birth of the Internet and explains why it was called the information superhighway. Also definitive was that this information could travel around the word at the speed of light, becoming available to millions of consumers who simply had to find it to quickly access and read it.

This also pioneered another pillar of Web 1.0, the search engine. Yahoo! was one of the early big players in this space, though multiple search engines started to emerge with the mission of helping consumers find content, as there was so much information available online it became a challenge finding specific sites. Thus search engines began playing an important role by aggregating and filtering information for users. Early ones like Yahoo! and AltaVista with their search portals were extensions of the overall portal and content aggregation concept. They were seen as one-stop destinations where one would go to find all the information that one sought on the Internet. Google was one of the first search engines to emerge solely and totally dedicated to search. Google's simple, clean home page was a clear and distinct move away from the portal approach to search that was previously dominant and the first to put search solely and totally at the heart of the search engine product offering.

The way that companies and organizations approached information distribution in Web 1.0 was still very much from a mass-market mind-set. They worked on the basis that they would continue to develop information and content that they thought relevant for the mass markets with which they wished to communicate and then publish and distribute it online. They believed online communication would retain the one-way and one-to-many flow of information of pre-Internet mass communication channels.

Technology

On the technical front, various elements also typified Web 1.0. First of all, Web 1.0 was technology-centric. By that, I mean the movers and shakers in Web 1.0 were people who could grasp the technology and who had technical acumen. Even at the consumer and corporate end of the wave, one found that websites were controlled by webmasters, people who had mastered Internet technologies and were qualified as gatekeepers of content that went through the site out into the wider cyberspace. They understood what the company wanted to say and what it did not want said. They would be the filters, gatekeepers, and masters of the websites and the people to whom one turned if there was a problem with the site.

Most websites had a webmaster at that stage, and those who could program or understand code like HTML and Flash were people who excelled in the industry as developers, designers, and webmasters. These were people who were at the forefront of satisfying the huge appetite that commercial and government organizations had developed for websites. This was effectively the beginning of the integration of the geeks, if you will, into mainstream marketing, the beginning of the IT department's movement from the basement into the front office of organizations. Early webmasters and people who understood the Internet and how to use it were seen as something of technical wizards. Lots of businesses sought to bring these skills and capabilities into their organizations, as is still very much the case today.

Also technically, Web 1.0 was about connections between web pages on machines. It was really about machines being connected with different machines and pages within those machines being connected with different pages on different machines via Hyper Text Markup Language (HTML). It was still very much a network of interoperating systems. It was not the internetworking of networks that led to the evolution of the Internet but more the internetworking of different systems.

In the early days, these systems were still very much closed. The big companies leading the market, such as Microsoft Network (MSN), America Online (AOL), and CompuServe, set up big online communities. They were set up as big content islands in cyberspace where people went to find information and entertainment. These spaces tried to control the user experience and exposure and keep users in their communities and monetize their activities. This idea of walled garden communities was a very typical Web 1.0 approach.

In so far as the Internet was about connecting machines, one of the big drivers of its growth was the proliferation of the personal computer. In the midnineties, personal computers began penetrating into people's homes on massive scales. The pervasion of personal computers and the birth of the Internet are somewhat synonymous, an interesting and rarely observed phenomenon. Prior to their spread into people's homes, personal computers were rarely more than game-playing toys or experimental systems for young academics. We had machines such as the RadioShack TRS-80, the BBC Micro, the Atari 800XL, the Commodore 64, the Sinclair ZX Spectrum, and other types of microcomputers. They did not, however, serve any real functional purpose in a domestic setting until the Internet. With the Internet came a massive proliferation of connected personal computers in the developed parts of the world, i.e., Europe, North America, and East Asia. These personal computers could connect with other personal computers via the Internet and its World Wide Web, suddenly making the connection of the computer to other computers more important than the computer itself. This was another important facet of Web 1.0.

So these computers connected with other computers through different systems, but the systems and operating systems were pretty much proprietary, as were the ISP systems. The only ubiquitous elements of it were the HTML and Flash coding and the standards used to manage the sharing of data from servers, such as FTP, FTPS, SMTP, HTTP, and HTTPS. HTML effectively became the global system that enabled all of these disparate systems to connect with each other via the World Wide Web.

Also technically, one of the key limiters at that stage was the processing power of the machines and the bandwidth that they had with which to access the Internet. Typically, most people had 56K modems then, and bandwidth was a big problem. At this stage in the evolution of the Internet, people generally had a faster Internet experience in the office than they did at home. People would have a T1 or T2 commercial or ISDN access point at work. Sizes of images and files became a big issue in ensuring those using 56K modems at home had good online experiences and didn't have to wait minutes or hours for files to download. A key capability for developers and designers in those days was being able to advise and optimize sites so that they could be easily viewed in low bandwidth consumer spaces.

In terms of the sites themselves, technically in the early days of Web 1.0, presentation and content were often one and the same. In digital terms, pages were static—i.e., they had creative and content that was "hard coded" and fixed. Toward the end of Web 1.0 period, an understanding of the importance of separating presentation from content became popular. With that separation, we then started to move to more dynamic content and toward database-driven websites whereby a consumer could request certain information and have it presented based on a request from a database. Content could be published to a site on the fly based on user requests so that pages moved away from being strictly static sites to dynamic data-driven sites. Another important trend that emerged toward the end of Web 1.0 was enabling customers to interact with content. In this sense sites could move away from being simple electronic brochures to being more interactive and engaging information-discovery systems or sales systems via e-commerce extensions.

This development trend peaked with the arrival of Macromedia's Flash 4 animation program with which agencies could produce complex data-driven sites with rich animated user interfaces. It enabled richer and more seamless multimedia experiences than plain HTML could give, producing sites that were much more fluid and animated rather than just static pictures and buttons on web pages. Flash enabled designers to give a much more immersive and fluid experience to the consumer. Toward the end of Web 1.0, around 1999–2000, it became possible to import data into the Flash front-ended websites. Stylistically this enabled designers and web engineers to create rich experiences that could still be dynamically driven by data as per the leading dynamic data sites within the HTML space. This was really the state of the art at the peak of Web 1.0, where we moved from static brochureware content to dynamic content through database-driven exercises with rich user interfaces, interactive content, and e-commerce sales engines.

In parallel to all this emerged content management systems, enabling sites to be developed in multiple languages for different countries. Style sheets were other innovations of this wave, enabling the presentation layer of the sites to be defined within the back-end code of it.

Programming was still the lead activity in creating websites, and programming code was pretty much proprietary at the Web 1.0

phase. The Open Source movement had begun but was still on the fringes of the corporate and consumer worlds. Toward the end of Web 1.0, the LAMP stack (Linux, Apache, MySQL, and PHP), the stable of the Open Source environment, came into prominence but was still seen as being unstable and volatile. Big corporations continued to gear themselves around proprietary programmed assets that were usually proprietary code written for proprietary systems.

The overall ethos of Web 1.0 technologically was about closed networks and closed systems, proprietary code and proprietary content. Processing power was key in the ability of machines to process information, and bandwidth was key in terms of how content could be consumed and the nature of the experience that consumers would have in the consumption of content.

3.4   Web 2.0

Culture

The first important observation with Web 2.0 is that it builds on elements that were established with Web 1.0 and develops them further. That said, there are some instances of conflict between Web 1.0 and Web 2.0 principles. In such circumstances, the Web 2.0 principles prevail.

For example, where Web 1.0 was about closed systems, Web 2.0 dictates open systems. So open systems supersede closed systems in the evolution of the web. On the other hand, whereas Web 1.0 launched HTML and Flash, Web 2.0 built on HTML and Flash. So while HTML remained a stable block of Web 2.0, it built on it with XML and other similar protocols. Though some Web 2.0 developments take the Internet in a new direction from Web 1.0, all build on the foundation of Web 1.0. It is important to appreciate this as we look at the Internet's evolution, as Web 3.0 will similarly build on the foundations of Web 2.0 and 1.0. So let us look now at Web 2.0 first from a cultural perspective.

Bidirectional Communication

The biggest cultural change of Web 1.0 to Web 2.0 was that mass communication suddenly became bidirectional. This was a world-first departure from the pre-Internet marketing communication paradigm. In Web 1.0 and the pre-Internet era, companies communicated one-way with consumers. All messaging went from companies to consumers, and very rarely did anything come back to companies from consumers other than sales. Analogously, one could say Web 1.0 was like a speech given by a company or organization that was heard by a large crowd of people. People generally could listen to the speech but had no real way of engaging the speaker. As such they were passive listeners. With Web 2.0, people suddenly had the ability to have a discussion with the speaker or organization and with each other in a public and accessible way. As such, where Web 1.0 was speech, Web 2.0 became a conversation. The people who companies, organizations, and governments were speaking to now had the opportunity, via the Internet, to talk back to those companies, organizations, and governments. Furthermore, their conversations with these organizations and among themselves about these organizations could be found and joined by anyone on the Internet. This was a fundamental shift from how companies and their customers had previously interacted.

This is tremendously important because hitherto the consumer had never really had a voice. The consumer never had a means of articulating his views or opinions back to the company, other than through very fragmented and abstracted means such as letters or phone calls to customer service departments that didn't make it easy for consumers and rarely got the exposure required by consumers to drive change. Web 2.0 changed this dramatically. It enabled consumers to voice their opinions and—important—it has given consumers a global network and platform with which they can voice those concerns or sing their praise. So suddenly the consumer has a broadcast channel with which to reach a global audience. This is a fundamental shift in the power balance between organizations and consumers, and Web 2.0 really heralded the beginning of this shift. Never before in human history can we find a scenario where common citizens were able to voice their happiness or discontent with an organization and have that message available to the world for consumption. Having this voice and potential audience has provided consumers with great power to affect the prosperity of an organization both positively and negatively. This represents a new social paradigm between consumers and companies and between citizens and governments, and it is a fundamental starting point from which to view Web 2.0.

Open Platforms

With the Web 2.0 world, the idea of closed platforms and closed systems began to dissolve. As discussed with Web 1.0, organizations like Microsoft, AOL, and CompuServe had tried to create walled garden communities within which they aimed to control the services and content to which their subscribers were exposed. That model did not survive the market crash of 2001, and what emerged from the first dot-com boom was a ruthless necessity for open systems. Openness became a principle of Web 2.0 development. Companies had to adopt an open policy in terms of data and information in order to be successful in a Web 2.0 environment.

Globalization

Globalization also became a key principle. With Web 2.0, the Internet suddenly became a platform through which anyone could have global exposure. Actually, whether companies were seeking global exposure or not, once content was available on the net, it was effectively available to anyone, almost anywhere in the world. So a sort of equidistance of markets started to emerge as a

Web 2.0 principle. The Internet did not establish the principles of globalization. Many social economic factors have been driving the move toward globalization over the past four decades, but the Internet accelerated this trend radically and dramatically. It also enabled small to medium-size organizations to have a global presence, a global distribution and communication channel, and a global sales and marketing platform. Globalization was thus another key element of Web 2.0.

Connected Consumers

Another important principle within the Web 2.0 phenomenon was that consumers suddenly became connected with other consumers. We saw in Web 1.0 that consumers were able to communicate around the world via e-mail. Aside from the huge scurry of spam and unsolicited direct marketing e-mails, e-mail was generally a channel used to communicate with people one knew. With Web 2.0, anonymous consumer-to-consumer communications also became prevalent. This was primarily done through blogs and comment sections on consumer sites, which picked up from the forums and chat rooms of Web 1.0. With Web 2.0, however, these enabled a much more significant cultural trend. This user commentary and communication began significantly influencing purchase decisions when people were seeking products or advice on purchases. It also started to influence the media and news space where people could comment on articles and on the comments of others about articles. This started a wave of user participation and user-generated content that became media worth consuming in itself. We started to see the emergence of social media, social networking, and social computing, where people began using the Internet to connect with other people who might be located in different parts of the city or country or around the world. People started using the Internet to find and connect with each other. The success of such popular social networks as Facebook, Myspace, and Bebo is evidence of the scale of this phenomenon. Web 2.0 is about a social Internet rich in user-generated social media. Deeply engaged consumers have aggregated in social networks in such concentrated and large numbers that corporations are now desperately trying to understand the whole social media phenomenon. They are aiming to develop marketing strategies that leverage social networks, as this is where consumers now are, and they are finding that people are not consuming the traditional mass-market media that they had previously relied on and dominated. Mass media are struggling to keep consumers engaged, and technology is enabling consumers to opt out of mass media advertising and communication. Many companies are consequently suffering a real disconnect with consumers and are finding a need to get involved with social media to understand how to engage with consumers in digital social spaces.

Media Consumption

Another key Web 2.0 cultural principle has been a dramatic change in the way that people consume media. As mentioned, interruptive advertising models that were successful in the pre-Web 2.0 era have been ostracized and culled in the Web 2.0 world. This is reflected not only within the World Wide Web, but it is apparent with the pool of technologies that the Internet collectively represents, including things such as TiVo, Sky Plus, and on-demand TV. These on-demand TV systems have enabled people to define when they consume content, again a really significant social change, both commercially and politically. In most countries prior to the Internet, governments could easily determine when the vast majority of the citizenship would be watching popular TV shows and could therefore broadcast political messages or get the attention of citizens at those points because they knew that they had so few choices in terms of what media to watch.

The advertising industry was driven by the fact that high-profile TV shows would be watched by large numbers of viewers at particular times. These time slots therefore commanded a premium in advertising rates, owing to the audiences they guaranteed. In the Web 2.0 world, the mandate from the networks in defining when people consume content has eroded dramatically. With the proliferation of channels and devices with which people can consume media, that power has now gone to the consumers.

> *I recall in the 1990s when interactive television first came to the United Kingdom. At that time I was working with the Central Office of Information, the UK government's main communication agency. I remember meeting many of the executives of interactive TV properties, trying to work through with them how we could utilize this technology to roll out government services. I became increasingly alarmed in discussions, as the key concern of the executives at*

that time was how to keep the Internet out of interactive television. They wanted to retain the TV commercial advertising model they were using at the time. They wanted to keep particular programs available so they could charge premiums for advertising slots in them and set advertising slots aside accordingly for big advertisers. It became clear to a few of us that if interactive television did not allow the Internet to penetrate it and be part of its overall offering, all that would happen was that the Internet would assimilate it and consume it, as is happening now. All the Interactive TV executives managed to do effectively was delay that by a decade or so. So in some sense they preserved the traditional TV model for a further decade, but we can already see the trouble facing television networks now and how the Internet is consuming them. Furthermore, there is still a huge revolution that is happening in how we consume media via Web 2.0 that is really just getting started.

So not only have consumers become empowered with a voice and a platform with which that voice can be heard, they are now able to decide when they will and will not consume media. They are now in control of what messages they consume and when they consume them. They are also able to broadcast thoughts on products to anyone interested in listening to them. This is having a dramatic impact on the whole consumer media space.

One media industry to dramatically demonstrate this is the music business. The web has radically changed the distribution and consumption of music, transforming the music industry's landscape. Two main things have driven these changes.

The first was music becoming available to the consumers via peer-to-peer networks. Napster was the pioneering system to enable this, and it became world famous for it. Napster's peer-to-peer system connected different people's machines in a global network, which became a global music database. This allowed people to share music with each other without necessarily buying it. Consequently people were getting music for free via peer-to-peer networks through illegal downloads of songs. As a result, the music industry was dented considerably and its revenues tanked. US music sales fell from $14.6 billion in 1999 to $10.6 billion in 2008, and Forrester Research predicts that 2013 revenues could reach as low as $9.2 billion. Napster, set up in 1999 by a nineteen-year-old college dropout, Shawn Fanning, became the center of an industrywide uproar and was eventually closed down following several record company-led legal pursuits. It was eventually sold to Best Buy following a line of successions from companies including Roxio and BMG. The rise and fall of Napster is well documented, but it marks a turning point in the history of the music industry. With Napster, the genie was out of the bottle. A vast content of music became available around the world for all consumers to download and enjoy effectively for free. This was a key element that was to change the music industry forever.

Another element equally significant and dramatic was that the industry's product became atomized, i.e., music media became atomized. What I mean by this is that it became more granular. The way the industry had been structured before was that record companies produced albums by artists. They invested in the artists, financed the production of their albums, controlled the distribution of the music through their distribution networks, and marketed albums via radio and other channels to promote the artists and generate returns by selling the artists' albums. Two strong marketing tools used to generate sales of those albums were singles and, with the birth and rise of MTV, music videos. The problem for consumers was that if you wanted to buy a song by an artist and that song was not released as a single, you had to buy the whole album in order to have it. If you didn't do that, you were kind of stuffed.

I remember having conversations with many music industry friends around 2003 about this very problem, saying that if I as a consumer want a particular song, then I ought to be able to buy that song. I warned that the industry would have to change to accommodate this basic customer need. Everyone at that stage was still focused on the illegal downloads and with scourging those Napster "criminals" who were basically arresting the rights of artists by illegally downloading music. One thing most music industry people failed to realize though was that Napster had exposed a weakness in the music industry's business model and was servicing it. My industry friends thought it was ridiculous to suggest that the industry would have to change to accommodate consumers' needs, and I remember telling them to watch, the Internet would eventually change it—as it did.

In 2005 along came iTunes from the highly respected Apple Computers camp, changing the industry permanently. iTunes was a significant and clever move by Apple, which we will be talking about considerably through the course of this book. Apple has done some significant, game-changing things in the advancement of the Internet.

The important thing to observe in the context of music consumption was that Apple pioneered a system enabling consumers to buy any song on its network as a single for $0.99. They managed to do this by collaborating with the record companies and artists and developed a distribution and sales model that benefited all parties. This was a seismic breakthrough. By atomising the music content of artists albums and making any song available for sale as a single via a legitimate and reliable online music store, Apple effectively revolutionised the music distribution model and dramatically changed the way that music was consumed.

That said, the iTunes music distribution model was not really a Web 2.0 model, it was a straight Web 1.0 e-commerce application. With iTunes, Apple gave consumers what they wanted: single songs or albums from artists of their choice, whenever they wanted them online. Apple also created a new business model for the industry. Any song could be sold as a single. Singles were no longer simply marketing tools used to promote albums; they were a significant business in themselves. The music industry was not prepared to change its model to deliver singles to consumers until Apple came along and gave them a vehicle through which they could do that.

So the key to the success of iTunes was two things: One, it gave the consumer what the consumer wanted even when the industry was not prepared to do that. Two, Apple made it very easy for people to transport and consume their music via the iPod. The iPod was actually what Apple was really focused on selling. iTunes was developed as a support application for the iPod. iPods came into existence before iTunes, but iTunes enabled Apple to provide a legitimate way for people to be able to find, discover, explore, and purchase music, in a granular way, song by song. Additionally, that music could travel with you on your iPod wherever you went. It was this combination of bringing commercial flexibility to consumers, leveraging the Internet as a content distribution channel, and bringing a state-of-the-art portable consumer electronic device that enabled Apple to not only revolutionize the music industry but also steal Sony's lead in the portable audio consumer electronics space with the iPod. So the iPod and iTunes enabled Apple to enter and dominate two new industries in which it had not operated before: portable consumer audio players and music. Apple was able to do this, if you'll excuse the pun, by thinking differently. This was the revolution that the iPod and iTunes led, and the music industry has not been the same since. Apple's iTunes has become the number one music retailer for all the major record labels around the world. It was able to deliver a global distribution channel to any artist or record label. Now artists are instantly able to sell content to consumers anywhere in the world from a single point of sale, bypassing the record labels' distribution stranglehold.

Social Media

With the rise of social marketing and the social element of the Internet, it has become important for companies to rethink content. Social media has driven companies to change their marketing propositions and the way that they communicate with consumers. For example, social marketing has exposed the inefficiencies of disruptive advertising. Consumers no longer have to consume advertising when advertisers mandate it, making the disruptive advertising model less effective.

Advertisers have had to learn to be careful not to intrude on consumers in their spaces, particularly in their social spaces. Facebook itself learned this the hard way when it tried to monetize its service by bringing advertising into people's feeds with the release of Beacon. We will discuss this later. The important thing to emphasize at this stage is that advertisers have to be very careful when entering social spaces. Advertisers cannot interrupt consumers' experience. They need to be invited and gain permission from consumers to be able to advertise to them.

Advertising is moving away from a push model to a pull one whereby advertising in itself now has to have some value to a consumer in order for that person to consume it. This is another fundamental shift from the way the advertising and marketing industry has worked historically. The nature of advertising itself has had to change, something advertisers are starting to realize. The most important thing is recognizing that the consumer is in control of what advertising he consumes, when he consumes it, and how he consumes it.

Referral Marketing

Another lesson to have emerged from the social element of Web 2.0 is the power in referrals. Social networks and social media on one hand are enabling people to have more robust filters from unwanted content, but on the other they are also enabling people to share content within their networks of friends and associates much more easily. As a result, the power of referrals is hugely effective in this medium. Studies show that 72 percent of people trust word-of-mouth referrals versus 15 percent who trust advertising.[12] Most companies that are active in trying to develop aggressive Web 2.0 strategies are now trying to find ways to have their loyal consumers and adorers advocate and become spokespeople for their brands in their networks. They are crucially trying to find ways to engage with consumers in nonintrusive and "pulled" ways that make consumers want to consume their messages and to equip them with the tools with which they can promote the message of their brands in their networks. So already we see a transformation in the way that a brand and its messaging is managed, moving away from a brand owner to consumers. In fact, the whole concept of brand ownership is somewhat skewered in a Web 2.0 world.

Brand Ownership

In the Web 2.0 world, it is the consumer who owns the brand, not the company. The company merely is the influencer. The company is the entity that can try to influence the way the consumer receives and perceives the brand. But ultimately ownership of the

---

[12] John Gerzema: The Brand Bubble

brand is in the hands of the consumer. It is the companies that give ownership of their brands to the consumer that are most successful in a Web 2.0 world. The companies that try to retain ownership of the brand and prevent consumers from being able to personalize, integrate, mash up, and play with the brand will struggle to achieve traction in a Web 2.0 world. The transfer of ownership of brand from company to consumer is a very key principle of Web 2.0.

Bloggers

An important group within this bilateral communication dynamic of Web 2.0 is the community of bloggers. Bloggers have become incredibly powerful people in terms of providing consumer-centric information. Bloggers represent a level of citizen journalism that's typical of Web 2.0, whereby, anyone with an idea or interest can write a blog and publish it online. Bloggers who manage to attract the attention of enough people who are interested in what they have to say can effectively become an entity or authority on their chosen subject. The reasons for which they may generate interest can range from a multitude of things. It might be the nature of the content, what they have to say, their style or humor, or it might be owing to a shared view, such as praise or dissatisfaction with a particular product, company, or service.

Interactive PR

It is becoming increasingly important for companies to woo bloggers, because they are gaining prominence. Also, based on the 1-9-90[13] concept of the Internet, i.e., 1 percent of those using

---

[13] This is a rule of thumb that can vary substantially across different markets and one

the Internet are creators, 10 percent are contributors, and 90 percent are consumers, active bloggers are influential in the web space as they are prolific creators of Internet content. As such, they often are epicenters of influence and centers of gravity in the digital space, being that they create a lot of the changing content that many other people on the web consume. Also, people often see bloggers as consumer champions—the Davids who fearlessly stand up to corporate Goliaths. So it has become crucial for companies to get on the right side of bloggers and to be able to influence them in a constructive way. It is, however, a delicate art. In some companies, bloggers are often courted as masthead journalists in newspapers and magazines are, owing to the influence and power they have in the consumer space. This can be a challenge for bloggers though, as they are required to maintain their objectivity to retain the trust and thus readership of their followers. Several companies have tried to have internal PR officers masquerade as bloggers and write seemingly external posts. These are mostly exposed though, resulting in significant reputational damage to the company in question. As such, the whole nature of public relations and corporate PR has changed very much as a result of Web 2.0. It has required companies to develop a new set of interactive competences, whereby they are able to respond to markets in ways that are influential though not dogmatic, top-down, or authoritative. They must be conversational and approachable in responding to content that comes from consumers and bloggers. As a result, transparency and rapid reputation management have become important behavior patterns and disciplines for companies to master so that

that is evolving along with the spread of Web 2.0 culture.

they are able to respond constructively and convincingly to situations that could otherwise be damaging to them.

From Websites to Web Spaces

Another key learning of Web 2.0 for marketers is that investing in large brand websites and expecting consumers to flock to them because of the magnetism of their brands does not work. Consumers are not compelled to watch companies' advertising on television as they were ten years ago. When companies build a website, consumers don't necessarily have a reason to go there unless there is something compelling for them, a difficult and expensive endeavor to achieve. As a result, smart companies are trying to pursue consumers in the spaces where they naturally go, which is more often than not social networking spaces. Facebook has over 350 million users worldwide who regularly spend time on the site.

Smart companies are trying to find ways to get into those places where consumers already are rather than spending fortunes to drive them to their own websites. This idea of "fishing where the fish are," moving "from websites into web spaces" is another big trend of Web 2.0. It entails moving away from corporate-owned websites and going into open, third-party-controlled spaces on social networks such as Facebook, Myspace, Bebo in the West or Tencent, Cyworld, and Mixi in the East, or within a promotion within MSN or Yahoo! in line with the groups of consumers congregated there. Companies now are much more humble in how they approach consumers. It is important for them to approach consumers on consumers' terms if their messaging is to stand a chance of being heard. Previously it was the companies with the biggest spend, the loudest voice, and the biggest mass-market access that would win with the consumer, but that is no longer the case in a Web 2.0 world. One of the key dynamics of Web 2.0 for companies is that it is a permission-based arena. Companies can no longer come in and throw their weight around or demand attention. That kind of action can be catastrophic for brands in a Web 2.0 world. They cannot demand that consumers read or watch such and such, or insist that consumers go to particular places. The Internet has become a space of negotiation, subtlety, and influence, rather than of control, dominance, and coercion that was more typical of the pre-twenty-first-century commercial landscape. Companies that understand this and that are truly consumer-centric will succeed in the space.

Groundswell

Another important Web 2.0 dynamic is the principle of groundswell. The term, coined by Charlene Li and Josh Bernoff in their book *Groundswell* (2008), suggests that an idea, message, or communication can come from one consumer or organization and grow in exposure by being shared with like-minded people who have a passion or interest around the subject area until it achieves a critical mass from which it can expand and grow till it becomes a highly viewed message or movement. Viral campaigning and social media typify this principle. Such media are often oriented around a small seed of people who get a message and distribute it to their networks. The power of the network, another important 2.0 concept, enables people to connect with other consumers, who then connect with people in their networks. This creates a snowball effect, and soon there is a massive number of users sharing and commenting on the media. Due to affiliations and common mind-sets and the power of word-of-mouth referrals, content can grow in terms of exposure and awareness at a phenomenal rate. If the content has traction and achieves the right viral critical mass with the right group of consumers or the right group of influencers, it can be an effective and efficient marketing tool. As such, viral and social marketing have become powerful ways for companies to achieve high exposure, with incremental spend. This typifies the idea of groundswell, which has been particularly powerful in the political spectrum.

We first saw this on a grand scale with Howard Dean and the organizations MeetUp.org and MoveOn.org, whereby Dean was able to mobilize millions of supporters around the United States using viral and social aspects of the web to congregate people around causes that were of common interest to them. These virtual congregations drove people to actually meet in the physical world and take action. Internet-driven social activism was something that we again saw used with great power and effect in Barack Obama's 2008 presidential campaign. Obama's campaign team was able to mobilize vast numbers of Americans to go out and take action on behalf of the cause. The team used the viral and social elements of the web to connect people and drive them to be socially active and campaign for Obama. Many argue that Obama's presidential election victory was hinged on his campaign team's prowess in using Web 2.0 technologies to mobilize and call American citizens to action. Internet-driven social activism was born in the Web 2.0 era. This is something that we will discuss further in a Web 3.0 context, where it's going to become a very powerful and prominent force.

Crowdsourcing

Crowdsourcing is another Web 2.0 concept based on the power of networks and the power in networks. Crowdsourcing is based on the idea of collaboration and having multiple minds examine a problem. It proposes that networks have intelligence and that great ideas and solutions to problems can be sourced from the intelligence within networks. This approach has led to many breakthrough innovations of the Web 2.0 era. A simple example is the name change of multinational consulting firm Arthur Anderson Consulting. Its new name, Accenture, was crowdsourced in an internal competition in which employees were asked to suggest a new name for the company. Anderson Consulting had unsatisfactorily paid several brand consulting agencies hundreds of thousands of dollars to suggest a new identity for the firm. In the end the name that was used came from an employee and cost the company the price of a two-week vacation prize for the winning idea. Crowdsourcing is another trend we will see grow and come into its being in the Web 3.0 era, but in Web 2.0 currently, we can already see models for the wisdom of crowds within networks. Crowdsourcing suggests that if you have one thousand or one hundred thousand people looking at a problem, you are likely to end up with something much more perfected than if you were to simply have five or ten specialists looking at it. This phenomenon is most prolifically represented with the wiki movement and with properties such as Wikipedia. Wikis are Internet applications that allow many people to collaborate and work together on producing something that's owned by the community of collaborators who create it. Wikipedia, for example, is an online encyclopedia that has thousands of contributors who add content at their own desire. The theory is if you have enough people looking at content as it goes onto the site, then inaccuracies, incorrect entries, and deception are eliminated. Owing to the massive numbers of people looking at these entries, the mass will be able to critique and correct any inaccuracies. There becomes a central sort of "democratic truth" that therefore prevails in the development of these properties.

The collaborative dynamic of Web 2.0 can lead to the development of great innovations. It can lead to great cross-discipline collaborations and the evolution of processes and products. It can also lead to different organizational structures and fundamentally drive an open, egalitarian way of working. Collaborative crowdsourced thinking is changing the corporate and social landscape in many ways. A book that explores this in great detail is Don Tapscott and Anthony Williams's *Wikinomics* (2007), which gives a comprehensive overview of the power of wikis and how they are changing the world in which we live.

The Long Tail

Another crucial principle of Web 2.0 is that of the long tail. This idea was popularized by Chris Anderson, editor of *Wired* magazine and author of the book *The Long Tail: Why the Future of Business Is Selling Less of More* (2008). Essentially what Anderson proposes in his book is that the Internet enables organizations or people to communicate with and sell to niches in a way that is unprecedented. He says that if you plot a chart of markets, you will have what resembles a dragon or creature with a large head and long tail. The head represents the large single markets, distributors, and media outlets, and the long tail is the ever-smaller niche markets. Big organizations have very big viewership, very standardized approaches, and very typical mass market and mass communication relationships. Typically they and mass media companies are most interested in the "head" of the dragon, i.e., where the largest single groups are. What Anderson reflects in *The Long Tail* though is, while those organizations and markets may have what appear to be very large communities and large amounts of people, there is an infinite number of smaller organizations—coming from the smaller large organizations all the way down to micro-organizations—that form a long tail of organizations and markets. Whether the tail is in retail, media, or another industry is irrelevant. The core idea is that this long tail of entities of smaller and smaller niches when aggregated represents a significant volume of consumers often larger than the large organizations or markets that form the dragon's head. It also represents a valuable group of targeted and aligned customers as opposed to a large but broad group of consumers represented by those at the head. In the pre-Internet world, corporations, governments, and organizations always worked with the head of the dragon. The Internet, however, enables organizations to service this long tail of niches in a way that has hitherto been impossible. Consequently they can be much more effective and targeted in engaging with consumers around issues about which the consumers are passionate and interested.

There has been some dispute among academics on Chris Anderson's theory, but again a very powerful example of the long tail model in effect was President Barack Obama's campaigning method during the 2008 US presidential election. Obama was able to outfund Hillary Clinton, who had the power of the Democratic funding machine, and John McCain, who had the power of the Republican funding machine. In previous generations, both would have easily outfunded Obama. What Obama was able to do by the way of utilizing Web 2.0 principles and Web 2.0 strategies was mobilize a long tail of supporters. He could get supporters to donate $10, $20, $50, or whatever amount they were comfortable with. When all of these long tail contributions were added up though, he was able to amass millions of dollars of support. And then, of course, with that funding in place, he was also able to go after the large institutions and traditional campaign supporters. As a result of these long tail dynamics, Obama was able to outfund all of his competitors throughout the election. Considering that he was an unknown senator with an unspectacular background and no major political benefactors who could give him this kind of economic or commercial clout in his early campaigning, this was phenomenal. There is no more poignant commercial and political example of the power of the long tail than Barack Obama's 2008 presidential campaign victory.

Personalization

Another key element of Web 2.0 is personalization. Web 2.0 enables people to have a much more personalized experience of the Internet. Consumers now expect that their experience should be personalized and tailored to them.

Engagement

Consumer engagement is also a key premise of Web 2.0. Consumers need to be engaged, as opposed to just simply communicated to as with Web 1.0. Since the interactivity of the net enables engagement, the challenge for companies is to find ways to present themselves and connect with consumers that will lead consumers to want to engage with them.

Lifecasting

Another concept that we're seeing in Web 2.0 is lifecasting. This means that people can broadcast the activities of their lives to their networks of friends or to anyone who might be interested. We can see this in places such as Facebook, where people regularly post photographs, videos, and blogs of what they are doing. In addition, YouTube enables people to post videos of their life, Flicker enables users to upload and share photographs, and Twitter is a significant space for sharing details of one's life and day-to-day activities. All of these applications contribute to the lifecasting phenomenon that we see with Web 2.0. Andy Warhol once said in the future, we would all be famous for fifteen minutes. Lifecasting in many ways has made that vision possible.

Life Caching

Following on from that, another Web 2.0 phenomenon is the concept of life caching. This is a means of people documenting their lives and having the highlights or activities stored in a virtual place that can be shared with friends, family, and associates and that can live on beyond the person whose life is being cached. Unborn descendants can perhaps view the cache in the future.

This is something we will discuss in more detail with Web 3.0, as it's a phenomenon that is going to gain much more pace in the next wave of the Internet than it currently has.

The Social Internet

We see that consumers are connected with each other in our Web 2.0 world via e-mail, websites, text and multimedia messaging, instant messaging clients, and social networks. We've also seen the rise of virtual worlds with Web 2.0, whereby consumers connect with each other and go to virtual places just to hang out with each other via virtual surrogates of themselves, i.e., avatars. Such virtual worlds have grown from online gaming spaces where people engage and play games with each other over the Internet to environments where people go to simply socially interact. Engagement and socializing are important Web 2.0 principles. Web 2.0 really starts to seed the idea of a social Internet. It starts to tap into the fact that human beings are social creatures. It begins to facilitate the social nature of human beings and to produce technologies that enable that. With Web 2.0 we find many people gaming, gambling, socializing, dating, and conducting all sorts of significant social activities with other people all over the world, making the web a much more social space than it was with Web 1.0. With Web 2.0, people are doing a lot of things that are central to their entertainment and emotional well-being with other people online.

For example, a huge trend of the Web 2.0 era has been the rise of online dating. Online dating has been responsible for more people finding love, marriage, and relationship partners than any other modern phenomenon. Online dating is a rich and significant element of Web 2.0 culture, enabling people to find partners so compatible with them that they can form lifelong and matrimonial relationships. This is a phenomenon that has not been well documented but that is transformational in our move from an analog world to a digital one. As we see global urbanization trends continue and more people move into cities and spend more time on their own single, this phenomenon is only going to rise. The Internet has provided people with unprecedented means of finding people for the most intimate of social interactions.

Consumerization

Another very important element of the Web 2.0 movement is the process of consumerization. Consumerization is basically the mass industrialization of applications and products for consumers in a way that brings the price of them down to a minimal, negligible, or free price for the average person. It is about products and services being developed and delivered to consumer markets as a priority over business and government markets. Consumerization has enabled people to have services at home that were previously very expensive or difficult to have personally. An example of this is e-mail. Hotmail, Gmail, and Yahoo! Mail have enabled consumers anywhere in the world to have unlimited e-mail and e-mail storage services for free. Computers themselves have also come down dramatically in pricing. The ability to have a very high-spec computer that will enable one to have a rich, immersive experience is being consumerized. The hundred-dollar computer is becoming increasingly inevitable based on Moore's Law[14] and

---

[14] **Moore's law** stipulates that the number of transistors on integrated circuits on computing hardware doubles approximately every two years.

this trend. Broadband access is still an issue in many parts of world, and even where it is available it is still perhaps more expensive than it could be. This too though is becoming consumerized, and we will see prices continue to drop.

Consumerization has been a real game-changing phenomenon, to the extent that employees within most global Fortune 500 companies are now able to have a richer and more engaging experience of the Internet when they are at home than when they are at work. The organizations that provide consumerized services—Google, Microsoft, etc.—have so many resources invested in providing these services to consumers cheaply that it is impossible for corporations to compete with them in offering the same level of access or storage capacity at a viable or acceptable price. Google, for example, has over five hundred thousand servers strategically located around the world, and in 2008 it partnered with GeoEye to launch a forty-one-centimeter resolution satellite. No Fortune 500 company that does not have servers or satellite imagery at the heart of its business model can compete with this. Nor should it try to. Corporations are now finding themselves in the Web 2.0 world, where their systems are clunky, slow, and restrictive to their employees. Employees are now finding it challenging to perform tasks while they are at work because the systems are so slow and restricted. They can have better experiences at home. In many corporations, marketing personnel cannot see websites they have created for the organization within the corporation's firewall. Consumerization is therefore a major cultural change in the relationship of the work and home environments and is changing the way that we can work. It is also changing the way that people can consume information and is putting the heart and impetus of the digital revolution in the consumer's hands and space. Consumerization heralds the point that the digital revolution is a consumer revolution. It is making it more difficult for companies to continue to operate with twentieth-century models while being effective in engaging and connecting with their consumers and employees in a twenty-first-century world.

Citizen Journalism

Another important trend that we have seen in the Web 2.0 space is citizen journalism. The network effects of the Internet, with people being connected with other people via their networks and with very few degrees of separation, makes for an efficient infrastructure for spreading information at rapid rates. This, combined with the rapid payoff seen with the groundswell effect, has led to a rich wave of citizen journalism. People all over the world have become major contributors to covering news events. Some of this is in alignment with major media channels, with properties such as Sky News, CNN, and the BBC embracing this idea and empowering consumers to contribute to the corporate retail news infrastructure. Some of it is autonomous, where citizens just report by blogs and within their social networks things that are happening in their community. These stories can get picked up by the major media or can become viral in themselves and gain traction and exposure among the Internet community. The seeds of this form of citizen journalism were sewn with Web 2.0, but it is a phenomenon that we are going to see expand dramatically in the Web 3.0 world.

It is a big shift away from the Web 1.0 and pre-Internet world of centralized news distribution and journalism.

Search Engine Marketing

Another important change from Web 1.0 to Web 2.0 has been the importance of search engine marketing and search engine optimization. As the information held on the Internet has become so prolific, the importance of search engines in finding information and data has become paramount for consumers. Now that many companies are actively engaged in e-commerce, search engine optimization has become even more important, as something in the region of 70 percent of e-commerce transactions begin with a search within a search engine. Even companies that do not sell products online still find it vitally important to be visible on search engines to drive people to information on their brands, products, and services on their websites. Search engine marketing has become the number one spend area in online marketing as a result of this. So the importance of content being optimized so that search engines can find it and rank it highly has become incredibly important. This is changing the way that content is structured and placed over the Internet. We are now at a point with the technology where content with rich media, video, music, and animation can be optimized so search engines can find it. This has not always been the case and was a bit of an obstacle to search engine marketing for some companies in the early Web 2.0 phases.

Internet-Generated Entertainers

And finally with Web 2.0 culture, we have seen the rise of Internet-generated superstars. The Arctic Monkeys were the first band to go to number one in the United Kingdom strictly from online sales. Soulja Boy, a US artist, also become a household name as a result of launching himself through a music video he distributed virally online. He became a Billboard 100 artist with his first album released and marketed online. Culturally we are now starting to see superstars and cultural icons emerge from the Internet, and there are online interactive shows such as the *KateModern* and *lonelygirl15* shows that have come from the Internet and expanded into the mainstream. *Lonelygirl15* generated more than 1.5 million viewers per week and reportedly achieved 35 million views between its first episode and season finale. Web 2.0 is placing digital media at the heart of the whole media ecosystem and, owing to the social nature of the medium itself, is starting to become the most significant and powerful means of starting cultural, political, and commercial movements.

Commerce

Web 2.0 has brought about a tremendous change in the commercial landscape. As we have seen in the previous section, consumers have become much more empowered. They have also become much more widely connected. In doing so, they have gained potency in terms of their ability to damage or support an organization. So a real network effect is visible and palpable in the consumer space now. Owing to this network effect, from a marketing perspective organizations can create content—such as short videos, for example—that can be distributed as viral media to a small group of people and then spread at phenomenal pace. The network effect of the 2.0 Web can lead to the rapid dissemination of information and content. This can be to a company's advantage, as in the case of the viral campaigns we have discussed, or to their disadvantage, such as when negative stories travel quickly around the web and cause reputational damage. This is something organizations have to contend with.

C2C2B Business Models

Web 2.0 has also brought new business models. For example, the consumer-to-consumer-to-business model (C2C2B) is becoming increasingly prominent. An organization that typifies this model is Facebook. Facebook effectively came into existence by providing consumer-to-consumer services to consumers. As a result of its volume of consumers and their level of engagement, Facebook quickly became an attractive property to businesses keen to market their brands to its users.

So Facebook was not a business-to-consumer property but a consumer-to-consumer property that eventually became a consumer-to-business property, and back to consumers again via a business-to-consumer model. This is a very typical Web 2.0 model that didn't exist prior to the rise of the Internet. Owing to Facebook's vast user base of now over 350 million subscribers, in 2007 Microsoft bought a 1.6 percent stake in the company for $240 million, giving the company a value of $15 billion even though it had only $150 million in revenue at the time. The rise of the Internet and Web 2.0 has meant that organizations can achieve tremendous market capitalization in a very short period based on the audiences they can amass and the level of engagement they can demonstrate that the audience has with their property. Google is currently valued at $180 billion in market capitalization after its 2004 IPO, yet is only eleven years old, a very young company by any standard.

Facebook has [had not at the time of writing] not gone public yet; it is still a privately held company. But it was also valued as a $15 billion company. So the ability to achieve rapid value is another element that Web 2.0 has accorded companies.

User-Generated Content and Consumer Empowerment

As we have discussed, from a corporate commercial perspective, one of the big changes in the Web 2.0 mind-set has been that companies have had to learn to empower consumers or to recognize that consumers are very much in control of the marketplace. This is not something dramatically new. In the 1980s, most management theorists and management schools were teaching the importance of being market driven and market led, and most organizations by the early '90s were proposing to be market-led organizations. The difference was that the Internet, and Web 2.0 particularly, placed companies in a position where consumer-centricity or lack of it became evident. In the Web 2.0 world, it is easy to see whether companies are indeed consumer-centric and whether they do listen to their customers, as consumers now have a means of articulating their thoughts and sharing them with other consumers and exposing companies that are not what they claim to be. Not only have consumers become central to the survival of a business, they have become empowered. So, the relationship between a company and its consumers changed, and no longer are companies able to dictate and control how their brands are received in the marketplace or how their reputations are projected. This has become the property of the consumer, who has become able to broadcast views of a company and views of a brand, whether positive or negative. This is a fundamental shift in the relationship between companies and markets. Companies no longer control or own their brands. Companies that wish to be successful in the Web 2.0 world have understood that they need to relinquish ownership of the brand and pass it on to consumers. Of course, risks are associated with how companies do this, and companies are rightfully concerned about promoting their brand messages in such an open context and climate. There are, however, clever ways to achieve brand objectives in Web 2.0 environments while loosening the rights around brand components in ways that enable users to engage with them. Web 2.0 effectively calls for companies to allow consumers to play with their brands' assets, to mash them up, to vandalize them in a sense, or to play with them and distort them—to personalize them in a way that gives people a sense of ownership and engagement. Web 2.0 has taught companies that this is a powerful means of driving adoration. When companies allow people to interact, play, personalize, and reinterpret brands for themselves, they become powerful advocates of that brand. They champion that brand in their networks, particularly when the brand represents a value they support or wish to project about themselves. Conventional wisdom, however, teaches companies to be afraid of this, as it involves them no longer being in control of the way that the brand is defined and how brand messaging is promulgated across the web.

One of the interesting lessons from Barack Obama's presidential campaign, in terms of how to do this effectively, is the idea of atomizing elements of the brand. The idea here is that, rather than presenting a brand as a holistic, complex set of messages and principles, one should distill the brand down to core concepts and messages that are smaller and more granular than the overall big-brand concept.

By way of doing this, those individual components of the brand can be disseminated, and people can play around with them without diluting the core essence of those brand elements. Consumers can then be enabled to reassemble those components in different ways, so that the direction and ethos of the brand is maintained but much more loosely than before. This is the key to success in terms of allowing brands and intellectual assets to be open in the digital space. Web 2.0 demands that assets are open, that they be made available online in a way that people can play with them, adapt them, modify them, and morph them with other assets or with other multimedia to create a story or something they feel is theirs and defines them. It is, however, a real change in direction and mind-set for companies to get to a point that they are comfortable with releasing control of their intellectual property and brand assets. Additionally, they are challenged with finding a way to do it that enables some of the essence of their brands to stay intact while still enabling people to engage, personalize, and take charge of those brand assets sufficiently for them to feel a sense of ownership.

This has been another significant change in the commercial impact of Web 2.0. Again, at its heart is this awareness that companies need to follow consumers. When we look at the previous Web 1.0 world, companies were creating their own websites and trying to get consumers to come into their world, into their properties, and into their brands. But progressive companies have understood with Web 2.0 the challenge is to get out into the web space, to actually go where consumers congregate. So the consumer has become like the Pied Piper, and the companies have become like the kids, following him diligently. Companies now have to pay attention to where consumers are going, and they must follow them on the consumers' own terms. More and more people are starting to understand this and engage with companies on that basis.

Virtual Currencies

Another commercial element of Web 2.0 has been the emergence and rise of virtual currencies. This phenomenon originated within the gaming world, whereby gamers could achieve credits they could use to acquire virtual inventory and assets via virtual exchange systems. These gaming environments eventually evolved into virtual worlds, such as Second Life, Forterra, Cyworld, MapleStory, Nurian, and HiPiHi, with exchanges enabling subscribers to exchange real-world currencies with virtual currencies and vice versa. This meant that people could go into virtual worlds and run virtual businesses and transfer virtual profits from that business into the real world, in real currencies. Second Life particularly came to fame via this, with the case of Anshe Chung, who became the first real-world US-dollar millionaire from selling virtual real estate in Second Life with Linden Dollars (L$).

Virtual goods is a multibillion-dollar industry. In 2008, over $580 million was invested in virtual goods-related businesses. Asia leads the world in this industry, generating over $7 billion per annum in revenues from the sale of virtual goods, about seven times the number for the United States. Historically, virtual goods have presented Asian online game publishers with a means of monetizing their products. So dramatic and significant has been this particular trend that certain governments have reacted against it. The Chinese government, for example, has banned the exchange of virtual currencies outside their native virtual worlds, stating that these currencies are a threat to global economic stability. It is important to recognize that the Chinese government understands that this is a phenomenon that can become significant in global geo-economics. Some virtual currencies— Linden Dollars, for example—have a higher exchange rate with US dollars than many physical-world currencies of emerging nations. Linden Dollars effectively trade at L$250 per US$1. Many countries have currencies that trade for less. The fact that these currencies are virtual does not necessarily make them any less meaningful than those of real-world states. We are now starting to see organizations study economic trends within virtual worlds to understand macroeconomic trends in the physical world.

The Mobile Internet

With Web 2.0 we are also starting to see a mobile Internet emerge around the world. This is having dramatic impacts on the emerging markets and countries of the world, perhaps most poignantly through mobile banking. Mobile banking and the idea of digital payment and digital transactions is another technology that has been seeded in Web 2.0 but will come into full bloom with Web 3.0. The Internet has seeded the idea of paying for things through mobile phones with mobile banking systems. This has been particularly successful and dramatic in developing parts of the world, especially in Africa and Asia. Whole rural communities have become engaged and economically active via mobile phones, mobile banking, and mobile payment systems. In many parts of southern and eastern Africa, the mobile phone is a means of transferring money from one part of the country to another. Citizens in cities can send money to family, friends, or dependents in rural areas as digital transfers via mobile, text-based systems. Those recipients can then take the electronic credits they receive to post offices and other municipal offices and change them for money. This is a powerful model in enabling a transactive layer between urban and rural communities in these nations, and we are starting to see dramatic changes in business and commercial landscapes as a result of mobile Internet and mobile banking. Mobile phones and Web 2.0 technologies are enabling farmers in rural areas to get instant information about the market, such as levels of sales, prices, and what crops are in demand in which parts of the country, enabling them to be much more efficient with the distribution and sales of their produce. We can see really dramatic changes in the commercial landscape, both at rural and urban levels, in many parts of the emerging world via mobile phones and Web 2.0 communication facilities.

Information

So we can see that the Web 2.0 era has represented a significant cultural and commercial change in the way that we operate compared with the Web 1.0 era, where the Internet was introduced, and the pre-Internet world that came before that. We also see a lot of changes in the dynamic of the web from 1.0 to 2.0.

Openness

Web 2.0 has fundamentally called for an openness, looseness, and fluidity of thinking from designers, developers, and managers. It has meant that we have had to be open with information, use open development models, be open-minded, use open systems, be open to having our brands reinterpreted and played with by consumers, be open to ideas coming from crowds, be open to new business models, and be open to trying things. Successful Web 2.0 models have been those that open data to the world, and the most successful Web 2.0 information models have been those that use open data systems to continuously enrich their data. A great example of this is Amazon. Amazon is truly representative of a typical Web 2.0 company. Amazon came to fame from selling books over the Internet. One of its key resources was having all its books documented or indexed with the ISBN code, which is the international code system used to identify most books that are still in print. Like competitors such as Barnes & Noble, Amazon's original database came from ISBN registry provider R. R. Bowker. Amazon, however, relentlessly enhanced this data, adding publisher-supplied details such as cover images, tables of contents, indexes, and sample material to its database of books. Even more important, it harnessed its users to annotate the data, leveraging its network of customers. Where Amazon excelled though was with out-of-print or hard-to-find books that did not have ISBN numbers. Amazon created its own proprietary identifier—the ASIN number—that corresponds to the Bowker ISBN where one is present but creates an equivalent namespace for books without one. As a result, Amazon's databases have become richer than the Bowker global ISBN database, so much so that after ten years, Amazon, not Bowker, became the primary source for bibliographic data on books and the most reliable reference source for scholars, librarians, and consumers. Opening data and enabling the data to enrich and grow repeatedly is a crucial Web 2.0 principle. Another organization that has done this very well is Google, with its Google Maps facility. Google created a platform allowing people to combine information and photographs with GPS data on any coordinates anywhere in the world, becoming a powerful and reliable mapping service.

Google was not the first company to provide GPS-based mapping services. Companies such as MapQuest, NAVTEQ, and Tele Atlas provided this service before Google. Where MapQuest and the others failed to understand the power of Web 2.0 and simply operated a Web 1.0 model, though, was in failing to take their core data and continuously enriching it further. Google, on the other hand, understood that by enabling people to combine or "mash up" that data, to add more information and more content to that data, it was building a continuously enriching database. Consequently, Google Maps has become the market-dominating tool. This tool has become so powerful that Google has recently launched a navigation system, Google Navigation, which is poised to blow current navigation systems such as Garmin and TomTom out of the market because it provides a richer pool of geo data about locations. Not only does it provide GPS data but it also provides points of interest, references, and photographs that people have taken and anchors them to specific locations. The Google database has grown more richly than any of the other previous mapping databases because Google has exploited the Web 2.0 principle of collecting data, making it available with open standards, and enabling people to enrich that data continuously. We can see that having an ever-enriching dataset has enabled Google to introduce new products and services to the market, taking it into new industries and new revenue streams. As an information strategy, ever-enriching datasets are a key Web 2.0 information management principle.

Syndication

Syndication is another important informational dynamic of Web 2.0. RSS[15] is probably the most powerful and popular method of this. Syndication enables people to select information feeds that are of interest to them. Anytime that information feed is updated, people automatically get updated versions of the feed's information. This "pull" as opposed to "push" method of information distribution has become a critical principle of Web 2.0 and has facilitated the transition of power from corporations and brands to consumers. It means consumers can opt to pull in information of interest to them when they want it, as opposed to having that information pushed to them when they do not want

---

[15] Really Simple Syndication

it, or as opposed to them having to go and regularly seek out the information. RSS and syndication mean people can opt into particular information feeds and get regular updates on a daily, hourly, or whatever basis they are comfortable with. This is an important transformation in the way that people consume information via Web 2.0.

Dynamic Content

Another element that sits along similar lines in the evolution of information distribution with Web 2.0 is the idea of dynamic content. Web 1.0 was about producing web pages with content that was somewhat static, or "hard-coded" as it is described in the industry. This meant websites would be coded with whatever information was available, and a webmaster would be required to go in and update that information should it change. One of the key advances with the Web 2.0 movement was the separation of data and presentation or layout. Consequently web designers could keep a web layout or design the same and pull information and content to pages from different databases in a dynamic way. This important information trend of Web 2.0 enabled the creation of dynamic content, which meant that real-time services such as flight or traffic information and other forms of dynamic content could be brought into web pages as required by a system and be updated regularly.

Technology

I hope what I have outlined in this chapter gives a good overview of the cultural, commercial, and informational changes represented by the Web 1.0 and Web 2.0 waves of the Internet. To wrap up, we will look at the technology principles of Web 2.0 versus Web 1.0 to give us a comprehensive overview of the difference between the two waves.

Social-centricity

As I have stated, one of the key distinctions between Web 2.0 and Web 1.0 technologies is that Web 2.0 technologies are socially-centric. They have become about connecting people with people and enabling people to get the content they want, when they want it, and how they want it. Two elements are at play here. The first is consumer-centricity, i.e., really thinking about how to get consumers what they want and how to get it to them as simply and quickly as possible. This simple principle has been at the heart of the Internet's greatest innovations. Putting consumers at the heart of everything and doing things in a way that made life easier for them and gave them more power has been the core driver of the Web 2.0 movement. Again as I have said, the digital revolution when you strip it down to its bare basics is a consumer revolution. It is a revolution about putting control in the hands of the consumer. Technologies that enable this thrive with Web 2.0. So website-publishing tools, user content-generating applications, blogs, wikis, social networks, open APIs, RSS, videocasting, podcasting, and instant messaging are all technologies that amplify and enable consumer-centricity.

Open Source

Another key technological trend of Web 2.0 has been the open source movement. Open source development—a term, philosophy, and methodology born of the Internet—has fundamentally changed the commercial and technical landscape of software development. The model enables developers with differing agendas and development approaches to work together in distributed networks where the intellectual property ownership of the source code used in development is open and rights free. A central principle is bartering and collaboration among developers, with the end product and source material used to create it being made available to the public at no cost. Open source development has enabled a vast community of developers and programmers across the world to create applications and services for consumers that are license free. The movement reached a tipping point in the late '90s, when the Chinese government adopted Linux as the operating system for all of its government departments. Open source has truly transformed the Internet by enabling people to develop license-free properties that are reliable, robust, and effective. This has tapped into the ingenuity within the human spirit and is an important movement, as it reflects that there is an inherent innovative spirit within man that is not necessarily commercially driven. It is not necessarily commerce or even competition that drives the greatest innovations in technology. The open source movement proves this. It also demonstrates the power of multiple minds working on problems and has shown that when barriers to collaboration and sharing of information are removed, great innovation can follow. It has had a seismic impact on the software industry and is now starting to spread to other industries, such as biotechnology and pharmaceuticals. We will see this model expand further to many more industries in the next wave of the Internet.

Perpetual Beta

Perpetual beta is a popular Web 2.0 concept and is one part of a two-part principle. What it effectively means is that in the Web 2.0 era, it is important to get an application or product into the market as quickly as possible. Once in the market, the product can be continuously improved and tweaked, thus keeping it in an extended beta state. The second part is the principle of "failing fast." The idea behind failing fast is that companies have lots of innovative ideas that can come to the fore within their organizations. Indeed, crowdsourcing, another Web 2.0 principle enabling the wisdom of crowds to be extracted and to feed innovation, has made finding good ideas even easier. Owing to crowdsourcing, which taps the natural innovation within organizations and inventive people, lots of ideas are constantly being generated. The principle of failing fast is that, rather than perfecting an idea to see whether it is going to succeed or not, it is important to get the idea into the market as quickly as possible to identify whether it has true market potential. If it does not, then the goal is to learn that as quickly as possible, abandon it, and then move on to another innovation, which potentially might have market viability. So the fail fast principle is effectively about being efficient with innovation and not wasting time with projects that aren't necessarily going to achieve traction in the marketplace. Coupled with this is the idea of perpetual beta projects. The perpetual beta principle means that a company can launch an application before the application is finished, giving an opportunity to see if the application is working and, more important, to get feedback from the network or community—in other words, to crowdsource ideas on how that application can be tweaked and improved. It leads to developing applications in a much more collaborative way and using the wisdom of crowds to refine and fine-tune those applications and to then release lots of minor iterations of a constantly improving product.

In the previous Web 1.0 and pre-Internet era, the approach to software development was that applications were developed to complete cycles, released, and then after relatively long periods of time, they had updates and new versions of them released to the market. Develop a product, launch it in the market, and then every six to twelve months have an upgrade of that product was the old model. The perpetual beta model is about getting to market a core product that is not finished and that is still a bit rough around the edges. Then you constantly refine it with tweaks and adjustments till you get to the point that the product is live, ready, or launched. As the principle states, the product is kept in a perpetual beta state so that it's constantly being refined and evolving, changing, and improving. It is never actually considered to be finished or perfect but is a constant work in progress.

Search Engine Optimization

Another important technological trend of Web 2.0 has been search engine optimization (SEO), i.e., optimizing content for discovery by search engines. In the Web 1.0 realm, the key thing was simply making information available. Search engines were there to find that information, but it was really only in the Web

2.0 realm, as the quantity of information became increasingly large, that companies and publishers started to realize the importance of making their information optimized for search engines. As e-commerce became a bigger part of the world's overall commercial model, search engines became an important channel through which consumers came to e-commerce sites to buy things. As a result, search engine optimization and search engine marketing have become important technical capabilities for publishers of content to master.

Broadband

Another technological principle of Web 2.0 has been the pervasion of broadband. Having high bandwidth capacity so people can download rich media content and get data quickly has been crucial to the progress of Web 2.0, to the point that we now, at the peak of the Web 2.0 era, have broadband mobile services and smartphones with which we can download high-quality video films versus the slow 56K modems of the Web 1.0 era.

Platform as King

Another important technological trend within Web 2.0 has been a move away from operating systems and programs to platforms. A fundamental Web 2.0 principle is that a platform always beats an application. The most successful Web 2.0 innovations have been the ones that can push themselves to the position of a platform. Removing proprietary barriers and opening systems up as much as possible are the keys to success here. Even when we look at something like Apple's iTunes, which is relatively proprietary, we can see that it is only when iTunes became available for Macs and

PCs in line with iPods becoming available for Macs and PCs that it became a music platform in itself. That is when it really flourished, becoming the dominant distribution channel and retailer for the music industry.

Likewise, it was not until Internet Explorer became available for any operating system that it became a major platform. Overall, we can see that the organizations that produce applications for the marketplace using open formats or APIs[16] that can be used by multiple devices and multiple systems, enabling them to become platforms for a particular service, are the ones that are most successful in the Web 2.0 space.

Peer-to-Peer

Another key technological innovation of Web 2.0 was peer-to-peer (P2P) technologies. Peer-to-peer technologies have been technically powerful for a few reasons. The first is that P2P technologies address a capacity-resourcing issue by making the resources of linked personal computers available to a network. This creates an efficient distributed computer resource model. Rather than relying on infrastructure and capacity to deliver content, it uses the network to establish that capacity. This is a progressive Web 2.0 model, exemplified by the company BitTorrent versus a more Web 1.0 organization such as Akamai. Akamai, which is still the dominant distributor of rich content over the Internet, has got to that position only by investing heavily in infrastructure, service, and capabilities in key locations. BitTorrent, on the other hand, has been able to compete with that

[16] **Application Programming Interfaces (APIs)** are protocols used as interfaces for software components to communicate with each other

infrastructure by simply connecting various people's computers together in an open network that enables the network to become the key resource in itself. That is one aspect of peer-to-peer technologies' power. A second aspect is that P2P technologies connect people with people via the machine connections that exist. A third trait of P2P technologies is that they make the resources of everyone in the network available to the whole network. Not only does this mean that the network has potentially infinite capacity but also that it has vast volumes of content that can be shared by all within it. So peer-to-peer technologies have connected people with people, removed capacity constraints by leveraging the capacity of the network, and made the resources or the content of the multitude of people in the network available to the whole network. They represent a long-tail phenomenon combined with a network effect. The sum of the content of every member of the network is much greater than any single entity's content. Peer-to-peer technologies have facilitated a huge amount of sharing and a huge amount of content being available on the net. They have also facilitated person-to-person connections, as well as addressed capacity issues with regards to the distribution of content.

Needless to say, one of the big challenges with peer-to-peer technologies has been the legal ramification of this sharing. There have been many efforts to clamp down and prohibit people from sharing proprietary and licensed content via peer-to-peer networks. In fact, there is legislation that has been introduced in France and the United Kingdom to effectively penalize people for downloading content via peer-to-peer networks by prohibiting repeat offenders from accessing the Internet. Peer-to-peer networks have been at the heart of the illegal downloading controversy within the entertainment industry since they arrived in the late 1990s. Nonetheless, they cannot be discounted as a serious technological innovation of the Web 2.0 movement, and while the legislative ramifications surrounding them are still playing out, new models are starting to emerge around these technologies that are transformational, legitimate, and empowering. We will start to see them coming into play much more with Web 3.0.

Mobile

A conversation around technologies of the Web 2.0 era would not be complete without also looking at mobile telephone technologies and mobile phone software applications. Credit for the recent transformation of this industry has to been given to Apple Computers. Apple created a new mobile Internet industry by converging the software, computing, and telecommunications industries via its iPhone mobile phone and iTunes App Store. This is a significant technological innovation of the telecom industry. What Apple did that was truly revolutionary was to separate cellular hardware technology from cellular software technology. It was the first vendor to do this. It then delivered to the market the groundbreaking iPhone, a hardware device that could constantly evolve and change.

Additionally, the App Store became an open community, enabling software designers to develop multiple applications with which consumers could constantly modify their phones. Now the App Store boasts over one hundred thousand different applications, with over a billion versions of them having been downloaded by people to date. Some of them are free, but others are paid for, thus introducing a new revenue stream to Apple and its community of developers. As such, mobile applications and microapplications have become a real principle of the late Web 2.0 era. The impact has been so dramatic that Apple became a leading smartphone producer with its very first mobile phone and established mobile phone manufacturers, such as Nokia, Siemens, and Samsung, have radically changed their model and created their own versions of App Stores. Also interestingly, this has prompted cell phone manufacturers to look at the computer industry and realize that there is an opportunity for them to play in that space. Nokia and Sony Ericsson have both introduced netbook computers and are now trying to move in the computer production direction. It's not entirely clear whether this is just gaming in terms of them strategically taking a shot across the bow of the likes of Apple or whether it's a strategic play in terms of them seeing that the worlds of telecommunications and computing are converging. Similarly, other computer manufacturers and software companies such as Dell and Google are now manufacturing smartphones or mobile phone operating systems, as we see with Goggle's Android, and are moving into the telecom sector as they too see the mobile-centricity of the next wave of the Internet. This is going to play out much more dramatically in Web 3.0, as Web 3.0 in many ways will be the mobile Internet, which we will discuss further.

So we can see a technological trend at the peak of the Web 2.0 era has been the separation of hardware and software in the telecom sector, pioneered by Apple with the iPhone, resulting in the cell phone becoming a device that can grow, morph, and change over the course of its life, which was not the case for cell phones before. Previously when consumers bought a cell phone they simply used it until it died or a new model with better features and better applications replaced it, which they bought, basically discarding the previous one. Consequently cell phones had product life cycles of anything between nine and eighteen months. This was so extensive that disposing of and recycling old cell phones has become a topical ecological concern in many parts of the world. With the iPhone this changed dramatically. The devices have much longer life cycles. People can retain their phones and make them more contemporary by updating the operating system, loading new applications, and updating the content on the device on a regular basis. This capability drove one of the essential design principles for the iPhone's user interface and has been an essential principle of its go-to-market proposition. The virtual and touch screen user interface, the separation of hardware and software, and the App Store are the three strategic pillars of the iPhone and demonstrate why the device has been so transformational and strategically critical to the cell phone and Internet industries as a whole.

AJAX

We spoke about mobile technologies and the importance of them. Another major innovation in the Web 2.0 space has been AJAX-type technologies. These are technologies that enable content to be repurposed or reused within a Web 2.0 space very quickly. AJAX is a technology that enables web pages to present information while retrieving information from a database without changing what the user is seeing. This enables browsers to present information to users while retrieving more information for the user. This means applications can become much more seamless yet dynamic and much more intelligent without interrupting the flow of how people consume content. Thus AJAX basically allows people's web browsers to be more interactive and to respond much more rapidly to inputs. Sections of pages can be reloaded individually rather than as whole pages, meaning the user experience is faster and more fluid.

Mashups

Another major technology of Web 2.0 has been the mashup, an application that combines data, feeds, or functionality from two or more different external resources to create a new service or new content. It is usually done through an API. Mashups have become very popular in the Web 2.0 era because they allow useful information or useful applications to be produced by bringing content from two or more resources and combining them to present something that is useful to people. An obvious example is the Google World mashup we mentioned before, where people can combine location information with photographic information by tagging photographs that they take in particular areas with the geo-data. When someone then goes to the mashup, they can look at a map and click on a particular area and see a photograph of that area in a combined way. Mashups are a very typical and important Web 2.0 technology.

Folksonomy

The last major technology we'll look at for Web 2.0 is folksonomy. Folksonomy is a method of collaboratively creating and managing tags for content and information. This enables information to be categorized and contextualized by different people and be collaboratively tagged. This again is kind of like a mashup for tagging, whereby multiple sources can tag information, making that information rich and multidimensional. This trend will also become increasingly important in the Web 3.0 world, particularly in accelerating the semantic web.

Appendix 1: Draft Universal Bill of Digital Rights

Preamble

The Universal Declaration of Human Rights consists of de facto Global Citizenship Rights inalienable to all people of the world.

A Universal Bill of Digital Rights will help to make some Human Rights and Global Citizenship Rights more meaningful, tangible, and enforceable in the modern digital world.

Global sovereign entities established by Global Citizens for the purpose of monitoring, upholding, and maintaining these Digital Rights under the principle of popular sovereignty are essential for the meaningful manifestation of these rights.

The Bill of Digital Rights

1. The right to identity as an individual person and unique set of data. UDHR Article 6
2. The right to access the Internet and to interact with other entities, including any entity or entities that uphold or enable Human, Global Citizenship, or Digital Rights. UDHR Articles 26/28/15/27/14
3. The right to have private conversations and interactions with others and the right to use secure means to enable this. UDHR Articles 12/19/18/20
4. The right to protection from arbitrary interference with one's privacy, family, home, or correspondence, or from attacks upon one's honor and reputation. UDHR Article 12
5. The right to freely express one's views explicitly or anonymously. UDHR Articles 19/27
6. The right to ownership of one's identity and personal data sets. UDHR Article 17

7. The right to access one's personal data held by all third parties and to have it corrected if erroneous.
8. The right to control which third parties have access to one's personal data sets and identity data.
9. The right to have one's data removed from third-party databases upon the request of the data subject unless an internationally recognized legal need to maintain such data exists.
10. The right to hold third parties that hold personal data accountable for the secure and responsible storage of such data and for protecting it from potential abuse, loss, theft, or getting into the hands of a unauthorized third parties.
11. The right to full transparency on personal data held by third-party organizations and to have simple, easily understood descriptions of the purpose, nature, and duration of storage of such data.
12. The right to contextual constraints around data that can be collected by third parties, limiting it to the purpose stated for its collection. Any other usage or expansion of these constraints must require the explicit consent of the data subject.
13. The right to require notice and explicit consent for the collection and storage of personal data and the right to be notified in reasonable time if such data stores are compromised.
14. The right to require internationally recognized due legal process for government bodies and NGOs to gain access to personal data and identity information. UDHR Article 28
15. The right to require focused collection restrictions to consented or necessary data only.
16. The right to freely move one's personal and identity data from the person's home territory to another and to have the personal identity data held in asylum within an asylum-

granting territory in the event of political persecution. UDHR[17] Articles 13/14

17. The right to petition to a single national entity for any disputes or violations of this bill.

18. The right to use the principle of popular sovereignty to establish and support internationally recognized sovereign entities that with the people's consent monitor, maintain, and uphold Human, Global Citizenship, and Digital rights.

---

[17] UDHR: Universal Declaration of Human Rights article that the Digital Right supports.